Reviews:

"An excellent book for beginners and mid-level players. A very structured approach to the study of chords and their use in guitar music."
—John Baboian
Associate Professor of Guitar, Berklee College of Music

"*Guitar Chords and Accompaniment* is *essential* for any beginning guitar player regardless of the musical style being aspired to."
—James A. Cox
Editor-In-Chief, Midwest Book Review

"I have never found an instruction book that'll get a beginner up and going as quickly as this one."
—Tom Person
Editor, Laughing Bear Newsletter

"This guide offers beginners a gradual, step-by-step, *solid* introduction to open, barre, and slash chords, fingerpicking patterns, and strumming techniques. Suitable for public and high school libraries."
—Cleo Pappas
Library Journal

"*Guitar Chords and Accompaniment* helps you get the basics down cold, and then offers up several more lessons. Very insightful, well written, extremely helpful. It stands out as a book with a lot to offer. I give *Guitar Chords and Accompaniment* an A+."
—Alex Steininger,
In Music We Trust, www.inmusicwetrust.com

Guitar Chords
and
Accompaniment

by

Yoichi Arakawa

SIX STRINGS
MUSIC PUBLISHING

Published by
Six Strings Music Publishing
P.O. Box 7718, Torrance, CA 90504-9118, U.S.A.
contact@sixstringsmusicpub.com
http://www.sixstringsmusicpub.com

First Printing 1998
Second Printing 1999, revised
Third Printing 2001, completely revised

Printed in Canada

Cover Illustrations by Frank Foster

ISBN#: 1-891370-10-3

Publisher's Cataloging-in-Publication
(Provided by Quality Books, Inc.)

Arakawa, Yoichi.
    Guitar chords and accompaniment : learn guitar chords
and various accompaniment styles step by step / by
Yoichi Arakawa. -- 2nd ed.
    p. cm.
    ISBN: 1-891370-10-3

    1. Guitar--Methods--Self-instruction.   2. Guitar--
Chord diagrams.   I. Title.

MT588.A73 2001   787.87'19368
                           QBI00-901767

TABLE OF CONTENTS

ALSO AVAILABLE FROM SIX STRINGS MUSIC PUBLISHING
QUESTIONNAIRE
ORDER FORM

INTRODUCTION

Playing chords to provide an accompaniment to singing or other instruments is one of the most important and enjoyable roles of the guitarist. In all types of popular music, from folk, blues, rock, jazz, country to Latin, you are most likely to find a guitarist, if any, strumming or picking chords the majority of time he is playing. In fact, many pros will admit that about 90% of what he or she does in a gig, whether performing solo or in a band, consists of playing an accompaniment. So whatever your goal is, whether you want to play as you sing alone, jam with friends or in a band, or perform solo guitar, learning chords and various basic accompaniment styles will give you a foundation and powerful tools to help you accomplish your goals. At the very same time, you will find yourself having lots of fun learning and playing chords and different kinds of accompaniment.

This book was designed to allow a student to *gradually* learn various basic guitar chords and many basic accompaniment styles used most frequently in popular music today. The greatest emphasis is on how to hold each chord correctly and how to make the transition from one chord to another, an area many beginners struggle with. Also, some fundamentals are briefly given including guitar parts, tuning, basic notation and music theory.

Practicing and playing every day are highly recommended if you want to be able to play an instrument well soon. Try to find at least 10 to 15 minutes a day to review and digest the material. Do not get discouraged even if you cannot see the progress right away or even if you feel you are not getting any better. The progress varies from one individual to another. And it is only natural that it takes time to learn and master things you have never done before. Spend enough time, be patient and persistent, and you will gradually improve at an accelerating rate as you proceed.

One last thing, whenever you learn new material, *slow everything down*. Read instructions and follow each diagram or exercise carefully and *slowly*. Practice each chord and an accompaniment style *slowly*. This will ensure correct learning and help you avoid acquiring bad habits that would be hard to break later on. After you are comfortable with the new material, then and only then, gradually increase the tempo.

Good luck! I sincerely hope that you will have a great time learning some of the most interesting aspects of guitar playing by working with this book.

THE EQUIPMENT YOU'LL NEED

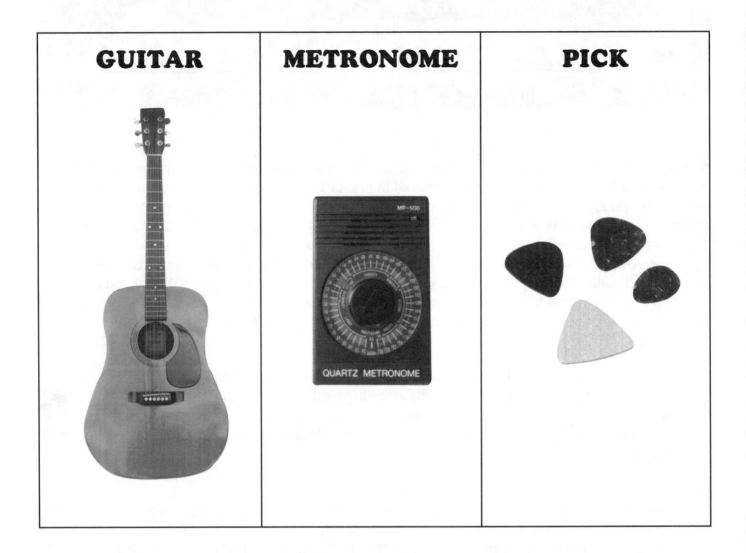

| GUITAR | METRONOME | PICK |

OPTIONAL EQUIPMENT

| MUSIC STAND | FOOT STOOL | CAPO |

CHAPTER 1
BASICS

Before you actually practice your guitar, let us go over a few basics. If you are already familiar with the material covered in this chapter, you can skip ahead to the next chapter right away. If you are not, take some time to study this chapter. It will help you learn the later information more easily and efficiently.

GUITAR PARTS

Do not get intimidated by all the names of the guitar parts shown below! The names are merely presented here for us to better communicate with each other. For instance, when the book says, "Position your first finger on the 2nd fret," or if you read "Keep placing your left-hand thumb behind the neck," you will know which parts of the guitar are being discussed because you have studied or referred to the illustration.

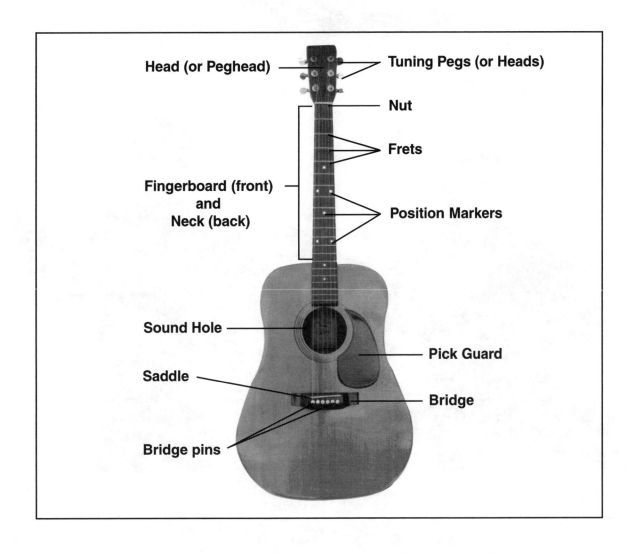

Head (or Peghead) — Tuning Pegs (or Heads)

Nut

Frets

Fingerboard (front) and Neck (back)

Position Markers

Sound Hole

Pick Guard

Saddle

Bridge

Bridge pins

HOW TO HOLD YOUR GUITAR

You have various options when it comes to the way you hold your guitar. The rule of thumb is to hold the guitar in whatever position is most comfortable and easiest for you. If you feel awkward or have difficulty playing at ease, that may not be the best position for you. Watch how people hold their guitars on TV, in music videos, or at concerts and then experiment. As a reference, some models are shown below.

HOW TO TUNE YOUR GUITAR

Each string of your guitar is to be tuned with a specific note or pitch. Although many other tunings exist, the most standard and widely used way to tune each string is as follows:

1st string = E	**2nd string = B**	**3rd string = G**
4th string = D	**5th string = A**	**6th string = E**

In the illustration below, the location of each note is shown as it appears on a piano or electric keyboard. When tuning, remember that tightening a string will raise the pitch of the note, and loosening will lower it. Tightening and loosening are accomplished by rotating the tuning head either counterclockwise (to raise) or clockwise (to lower).

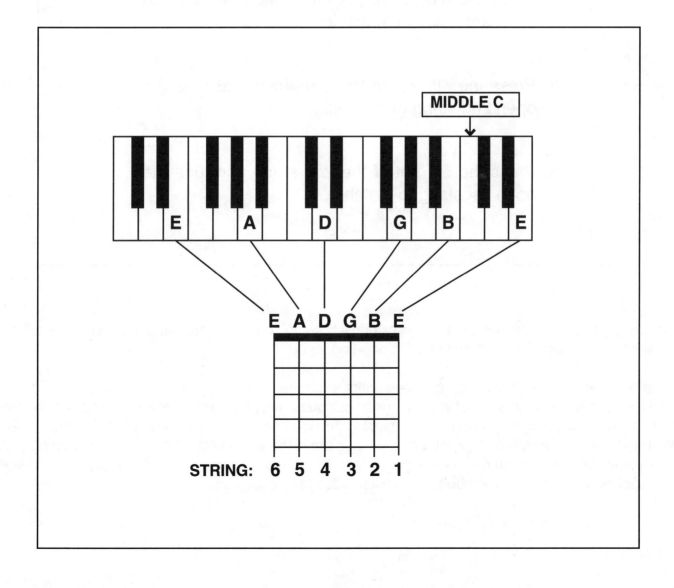

If you do not have a keyboard or piano at hand, here is another tuning method commonly used:

1. Using either a tuning fork or electric metronome which has A4 440Hz tuning pitch, tune the 5th string to **A**.

2. Next, press the 5th fret of the 6th string and tune it to match the open 5th string (*open* means you do not press the string).

3. Similarly, press the 5th fret of the 5th string and tune the open 4th string to match the pitch.

4. Press the 5th fret of the 4th string and tune the open 3rd string to match it.

5. Press the 4th fret of the 3rd string and tune the open 2nd string to match it.

6. Press the 5th fret of the 2nd string and tune the open 1st string to match it.

Notice that except for the tuning of the 2nd string where you press the 4th fret of the 3rd string, all the others have you press the 5th fret of the preceding string.

Tuning is one of the first hurdles many beginners encounter. Many of you may feel uncertain at first and it may take a little while until you can tune your guitar with absolute confidence and at ease. Be patient and keep practicing so that your sense of pitch will improve and the tuning will become easier. When you are not certain as to whether two strings are in the same pitch or not, loosen the string you are tuning down and bring it up slowly and gradually. Repeat this process many times and you will start getting a good sense of whether the pitch is too low or too high.

BASIC MUSIC NOTATION

Staff

Music is written on a *staff* which consists of 5 lines and 4 spaces between the lines. The lines and spaces indicate specific pitches or sound.

Measure and Bar Line

The staff is divided into *measures*. A *bar line* separates one measure from another.

Double Bar Line

‖ is used to indicate the end of a piece of a section. ‖ is used at the end of a composition or song.

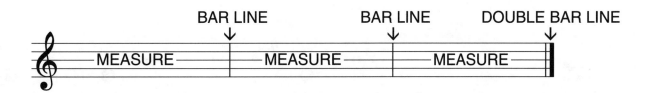

Repeat Signs

The sign :‖ at the end of a song or section indicates that the music should be played again from the beginning of the song to the sign.

When a repeat sign ‖: within a music is later followed by another sign :‖, it tells you to play the same music once more, beginning at the first sign and ending at the second one.

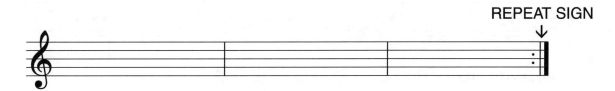

When you have repeat signs with two brackets marked by 1 and 2, play through the end of the bracket marked by 1 *(first ending)*, go back to the beginning and repeat. When you reach the first-ending bracket, skip it and go directly to the bracket marked by 2 *(second ending)*.

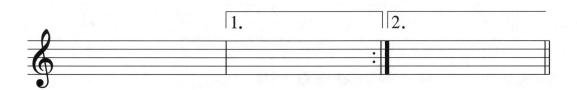

14

D.C. (da capo)

D.C., an abbreviation for *da capo* (which means *from the beginning* in Italian) directs the performer to go back and repeat the music from the beginning.

D.S. (dal segno)

D.S. is an abbreviation for *dal segno* (which means *from the sign* in Italian). It means to repeat the music from the sign: 𝄋.

Fine

Fine means the end of music. It is often used in conjunction with D.C or D.S. *D.C. al fine*, for example, means to go back to the beginning and repeat the music up to the measure marked *fine*. Similarly, *D.S. al fine* directs you to go back to the 𝄋 sign and play the music up to *fine*.

Playing direction: ❶ → ❷ → ❸ → ❹ → ❺ → ❻ → ❶ → ❷ → ❸

Playing direction: ❶ → ❷ → ❸ → ❹ → ❺ → ❻ → ❸ → ❹

Coda

Coda is a closing section of music, often indicated by such signs as ⊕ or *Coda* ⊕. Again, it is often found in conjunction with D.C. or D.S signs. *D.C. al Coda*, for example, means to go back to the beginning of the music, repeat the music up to the measure marked with ⊕ or *To Coda* ⊕, and go to the Coda section. Similarly, *D.S. al Coda* means to go back to the 𝄋 sign, repeat the music up to ⊕ or *To Coda* ⊕, and go and play the Coda section to finish up the music. If there are repeat signs between the beginning of the music and D.C. or between the 𝄋 sign and D.S., the music within repeat signs is normally not repeated the second time unless there are such indications as *D.C. (with repeat) al Coda* or *D.S. (with repeat) al Coda*.

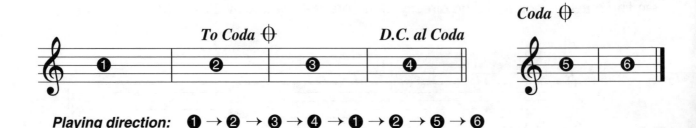

Playing direction: ❶ → ❷ → ❸ → ❹ → ❶ → ❷ → ❺ → ❻

Count or Rhythm

The majority of today's music is played with a definite beat or rhythm. The beat is a steady, regular pulse or count throughout the music that is just like the ticking of a watch. Musicians rely on this regular pulse whenever they play.

Pacing yourself with your metronome, tap your foot and say ONE-TWO-THREE-FOUR, ONE-TWO-THREE-FOUR….Notice how steady and equal each count is in time and speed. Your goal will be to become able to keep track of the beat as accurately as the metronome.

Notes

Notes are symbols that indicate musical sounds. How long you sustain or hold the sound depends on what kind of notes you are playing.

NOTES	NAME OF THE NOTES	HOW MANY COUNTS
𝅝	**WHOLE NOTE**	Played and sustained for **4** counts
𝅗𝅥	**HALF NOTE**	Played and sustained for **2** counts
𝅘𝅥	**QUARTER NOTE**	Played and sustained for **1** count
𝅘𝅥𝅮	**EIGHTH NOTE**	Played and sustained for **1/2** count
𝅘𝅥𝅯	**SIXTEENTH NOTE**	Played and sustained for **1/4** count
𝅗𝅥.	***DOTTED HALF NOTE**	Played and sustained for **3** counts
𝅘𝅥.	***DOTTED QUARTER NOTE**	Played and sustained for **1 1/2** counts
𝅘𝅥𝅮.	***DOTTED EIGHTH NOTE**	Played and sustained for **3/4** counts

A dot after a note increases any note value by 1/2.

Beams

When you have a group of two or more eighth notes or sixteenth notes, they are usually connected by a thick, horizontal line(s), called *beam(s)*. As shown on the next page, eighth notes are joined by a single beam and sixteenth notes are connected by two beams.

Examples:

Rest

Rest indicates silence. Similar to notes, how many counts or how long you *do not* play depends on what kind of rest symbols you have on the staff.

RESTS	NAME OF THE RESTS	COUNTS TO REST
▬	**WHOLE REST**	Rest for **4** counts
▬	**HALF REST**	Rest for **2** counts
𝄽	**QUARTER REST**	Rest for **1** count
𝄾	**EIGHTH REST**	Rest for **1/2** count
𝄿	**SIXTEENTH REST**	Rest for **1/4** count

Tempo Markings

How fast or slow music is played or *tempo* is indicated either by a metronomic setting or by an Italian (or English) descriptive term. A metronomic notation shows the number of beats per minute. For example, ♩ = 60 means that a quarter note is held for exactly 1/60 of a minute, or 1 second. The higher the number, the faster the tempo is. The tempo is slow if the number is low.

ITALIAN	ENGLISH	METRONOME
Largo	Slow	40-60
Larghetto (Lento)	Slowly	60-66
Adagio	Slowly at ease	66-76
Andante	Moderately (walking speed)	76-108
Moderato	Moderately	108-120
Allegro	Fast	120-168
Presto	Very Fast	168-200

Time Signature

At the beginning of every song, you see two numbers placed together as a fraction. This fraction is called the *time signature*. The signature shows us both how many counts there are in each measure and what kind of note will represent one count or beat.

The upper number : Tells how many counts there are in ONE bar.

***The bottom number:** Tells us what kind of note gets ONE count.

* A number is assigned to each note:
Whole note: **1**   *Half note:* **2**   *Quarter note:* **4**   *Eighth note:* **8**

Examples:

$\frac{3}{4}$: 3 counts in a measure and a quarter note gets 1 count.

$\frac{2}{4}$: 2 counts in a measure and a quarter note gets 1 count.

$\frac{6}{8}$: 6 counts in a measure and an eighth note gets 1 count.

$\frac{12}{8}$: 12 counts in a measure and an eighth note gets 1 count.

Pitches and Clef

A *pitch* tells us how low or high the sound of the note is. This sound is indicated by where you find a note on the staff. The higher a note is placed, the higher the pitch is. Conversely, the lower the note is placed, the lower the sound.

Pitches are named alphabetically using seven English letters: **A, B, C, D, E, F,** and **G**. For example, B is one note higher than A, while E is one note lower than F. What note is higher than the note G? The answer is the note A. These seven letters are the only ones used in naming the musical notes, and the same name repeats after every seven names.

You may be asking yourself, "OK, I understand there are seven note names whose corresponding pitches (or how low or high the sounds are) are determined by their positions on the staff. So where is the A note, C note, or D note on the staff? Where would a note be placed to indicate the pitch that corresponds to C or E or F?"

The *clef* which is placed at the beginning of a piece of music gives us a reference point for the placement of the notes. Different kinds of clefs require different locations of the notes on the staff.

CLEFS	NAME	MEANING
𝄞	**G** or **TREBLE CLEF**	Indicates that any note placed on the *2nd line from the bottom* will be called a **G**. The other notes are named alphabetically in reference to the G.
𝄢	**F** or **BASS CLEF**	Indicates that any note placed on the *2nd line from the top* will be called an **F**. The other notes are named alphabetically in reference to the F.

These are the two clefs most often used. Different clefs are chosen depending on the range of the music being written. For example, the treble clef is used for music for such high-pitched instruments as the flute and violin. Low-pitched instruments such as bass, cello, and bassoon call for the bass clef. In piano music, the treble clef is used for the upper staff and the bass clef for the lower staff. Guitar music is always written in **G** or **treble** clef.

Below you will find the name of the notes in each clef. You may notice the same letter names appearing in different places. For example, the E note can be found on the 3rd space of the bass clef and on the 1st line and 4th space of the treble clef. The same letter name repeats every eighth time and the notes are said to be an *octave* apart; they sound the same, but only higher or lower.

The pitch C written below the treble staff is exactly the same as the pitch C written above the bass staff. This note is known as **"middle C."**

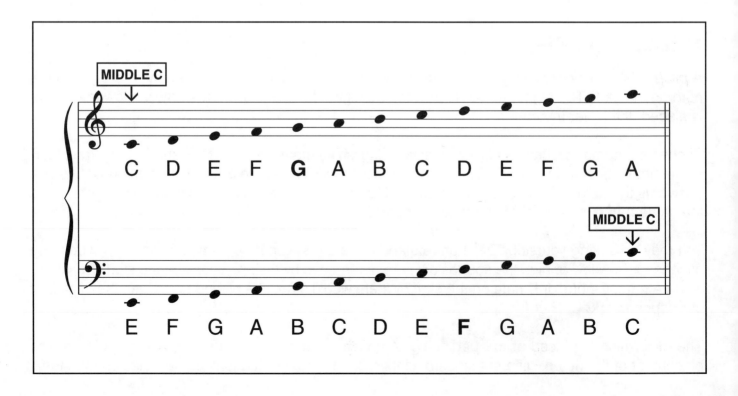

Accidentals

Half step or half tone is the smallest distance between two notes. On the guitar, a half step is one fret up or down. Two half steps are equal to a *whole step* which is two frets apart on guitar. *Accidentals* are the signs used to raise or lower the pitch of a note or to cancel such a change. The smallest change one can make to a note is a half step. All accidentals are placed before the note. In speaking and when naming a chord, the accidental always follows the letter name, as C♯ (*C sharp*), E♭ (*E flat*), A♭♭ (*A double flat*), etc. Below is a summary of accidentals and their meaning:

ACCIDENTALS		MEANING
♯	**SHARP**	Raises a pitch a half-step
♭	**FLAT**	Lowers a pitch a half-step
✕	**DOUBLE SHARP**	Raises a pitch a whole-step
♭♭	**DOUBLE FLAT**	Lowers a pitch a whole-step
♮	**NATURAL**	Cancels a previous accidental sign and returns that note to its unchanged form

Enharmonic Notation

Using different accidentals, the same sounding note can be written in several different ways. For example, C♯ is the same as B✕ or D♭. F can be also called as E♯ or G♭♭. Sounds that are the same, but written with different signs, are called *enharmonic*. The enharmonic notation applies to naming both notes and chords.

Key Signature

A *key signature* is a group of sharps or flats placed at the beginning of a staff immediately after the clef sign. It indicates two things. First, all notes on which the sharp(s) or flat(s) indicated by the key signature are to be raised or lowered throughout the music unless a note is cancelled by the natural sign or by a different key signature. Second, a key signature tells you in what *key* a piece of music is. (For details on *key*, refer to *Jazz Guitar Chords and Accompaniment* or a music theory book.)

Examples:

CHAPTER 1 REVIEW

1. Identify and write the name of the following notes:

F   _   _   _   _   _   _   _   _

_   _   _   _   _   _   _   _

2. Write the name and duration for the following notes:

whole   _____   _____   _____   _____   _____   _____   _____

4 beats   _____   _____   _____   _____   _____   _____   _____

3. Write the name and duration for the following rests:

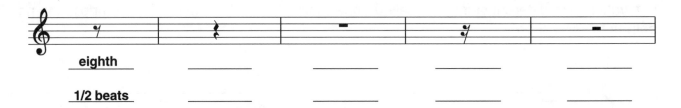

eighth   _____   _____   _____   _____

1/2 beats   _____   _____   _____   _____

4. Write the playing direction for the followings:

a)

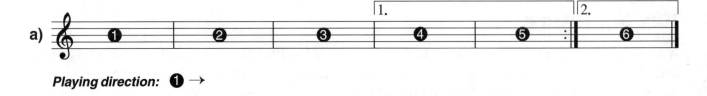

Playing direction: ❶ →

b)

Playing direction: ❶ →

CHAPTER 2
BASIC OPEN CHORDS AND STRUMMING

A *chord* is the sounding of three or more notes simultaneously. One of the most important roles of playing chords in music is to provide accompaniment for singers or other instruments. In this chapter, you are going to learn the basic, yet most-used guitar chords, called *open chords* and one of the basic accompaniment styles called *strumming*. Below are a few items for you to go over before doing the exercises.

CHORD DIAGRAM

A chord diagram or a chord frame shows a portion of the guitar fingerboard. Six vertical lines represent strings, from left to right, 6th, 5th, 4th, 3rd, 2nd, 1st. Horizontal lines represent frets. The thick horizontal line at the very top is the nut. Black dots placed on the vertical lines represent the locations at which left-hand fingers should be placed.

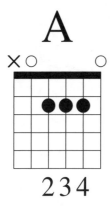

The letter above the diagram indicates the name of the chord.

O: Indicates an open string meaning you play the string without pressing.

X: Indicates the string is not to be played.

Each number below a string shows which left-hand finger to use to press each dot.

Each left-hand finger is assigned a number:

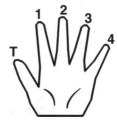

T: Thumb
1: 1st finger
2: 2nd finger
3: 3rd finger
4: 4th finger

SLASH NOTATION

Slashes instead of oval-shaped notes are normally used in a rhythm chart or when indicating strumming. Just like the note, a slash indicates how long or how many counts you sustain the chord. Below you will find the different kinds of slashes corresponding to the notes.

Regular Notation	𝅝	𝅗𝅥	♩	♪	♬	𝅗𝅥.	♩.	♪.
Slash Notation	⟋	⟋	⟋	⟋	⟋	⟋.	⟋.	⟋.
Counts	4	2	1	1/2	1/4	3	1.5	3/4

HOLDING A PICK

The use of a pick is one of the most popular and useful ways to play the guitar, especially when strumming. If you prefer, you can strum with your right-hand fingers or with a thumbpick. There are a number of different ways to hold a pick: some people use the thumb and the index finger, others hold a pick between the thumb, the index finger and the middle finger and yet there are other guitar players who prefer holding a pick with their thumb and the middle finger. Experiment with several ways and try to find the method of holding the pick that is most comfortable for you. As a reference, the most common way of holding a pick is shown below.

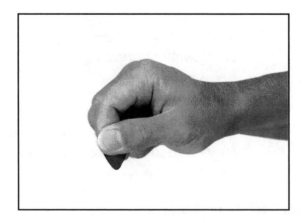

USING A CAPO

If you have some difficulty holding chords, especially the ones that require you to stretch your hand, a capo may help you press those chords better. Place a capo on the 2nd or 3rd fret and pretend that the fret is the nut or very top of the guitar. The narrower distance between each fret as you go down the fingerboard may allow you to play that difficult chord more easily.

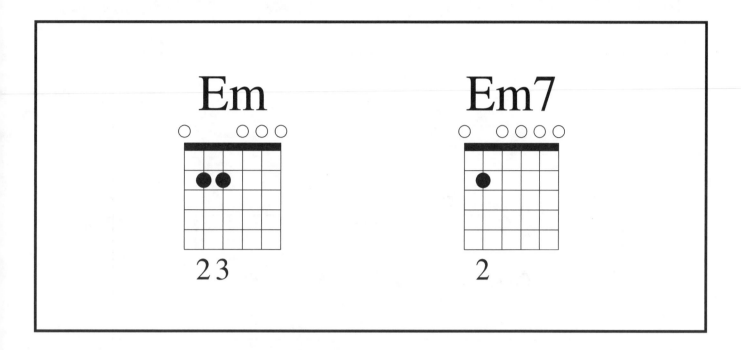

2-1

The Em (*E minor*) chord is the first chord you are going to learn. (Note: all minor chords are abbreviated as **m**; so E minor is written as **Em**, A minor is written as **Am**, and so on.) First, take a look at the diagram. Then as shown, use the 2nd and 3rd fingers of your left hand to press the dots. If this is your first attempt to play any chord, you may have some difficulties pressing each finger against the fingerboard. This is natural at first. Be patient, take a break and try it as many times as you find necessary. Go ahead and play the chord striking the 6th to 1st strings individually in sequence.

Here are a few things for you to keep in mind whenever playing a chord, which are true and applicable to all the other chords you are going to learn later in this book.

TIPS

1. Press your fingertips on the guitar fingerboard as firmly as you can.

2. Make sure they do not touch the neighboring strings so that the sound is clear without a buzz.

3. Memorize each chord by visualizing it as a *shape*.

Now, let's try simple strumming. The symbol, ⊓, indicates a downstroke, meaning you strum or brush strings from the 6th string to the 1st string, toward the floor. Set your metronome to a slow tempo that you feel comfortable with (around 50 or 54). Count and tap your foot along with each click: **ONE-TWO-THREE-FOUR, ONE-TWO-THREE-FOUR**, etc.

For the first strumming pattern, you strum the chord at ONE and hold the sound for 4 counts (ONE-TWO-THREE-FOUR). Repeat it as many times as you can until you can strike the chord at the right time with the metronome and sustain the sound exactly for 4 counts.

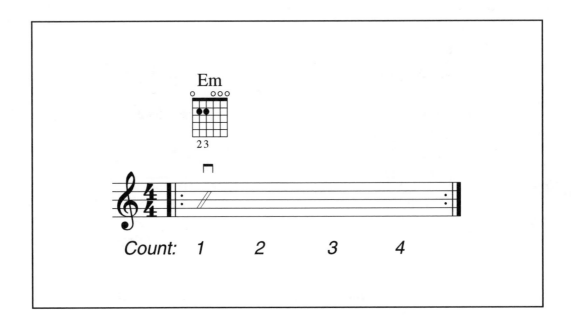

When strumming, strive for a steady, fluid motion. Your shoulders as well as the wrist and arm on the strumming side should be as relaxed as possible as shown below.

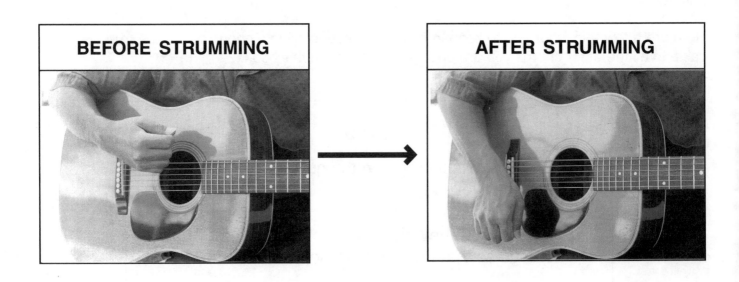

Next try the Em7 (*E minor seventh*) chord. As you'll notice, the only difference between Em and Em7 is whether you play the 3rd finger on the 4th string or not. The strumming pattern for Em7 uses two *half-note* slashes in a measure. Count ONE-TWO-THREE-FOUR in exactly the same manner as when you play Em. Strum the chord with a downstroke at ONE, sustain for two counts, then strike again at THREE, and sustain for two counts to complete the measure. Repeat this pattern over and over until you are comfortable with it.

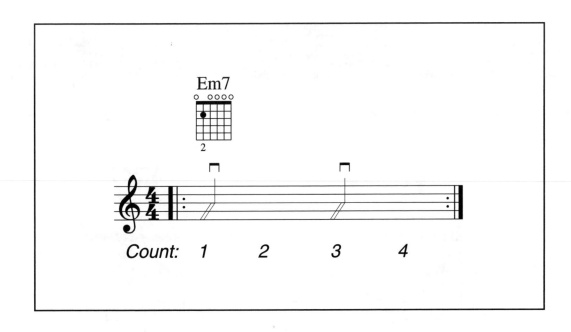

When you are able to play each chord on time with the metronome, try two chords in sequence as shown below. Strive for a smooth connection between the chords. Any transition from one chord to another should be as noiseless and smooth as possible. Note that when moving from Em to Em7, all you need to do is lift your 3rd finger off the fingerboard. Conversely, from Em7 to Em, just press your 3rd finger on the 4th string, 2nd fret. In both instances, do not move or lift your 2nd finger. Keep pressing it throughout.

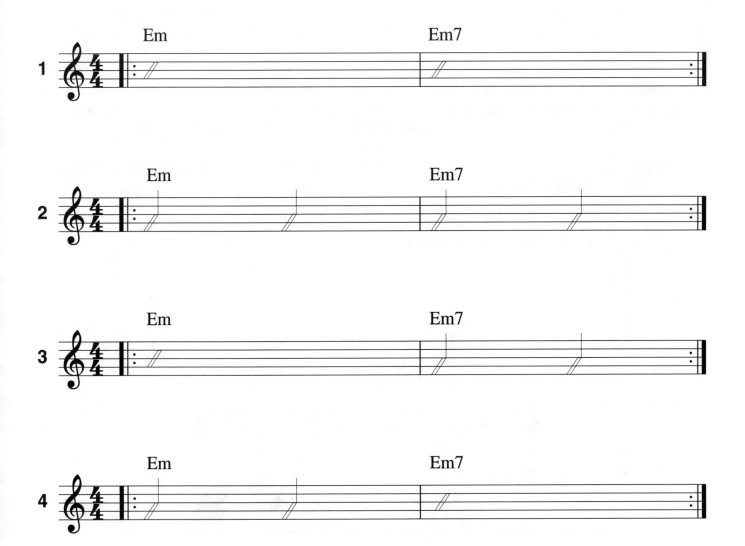

2-2

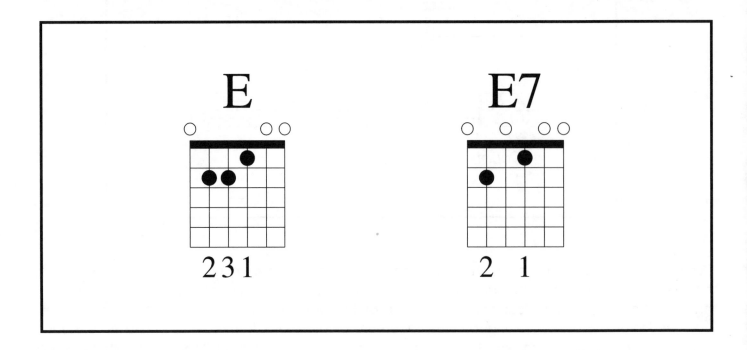

E and E7 are the next chords to learn. As you may have noticed, they look very similar to the chords you have just learned, Em and Em7. Press Em, then add your 1st finger on the 3rd string, 1st fret. You now have an E chord. Press Em7, then add your 1st finger on the 3rd string, 1st fret. You have the E7 chord. Once you feel comfortable pressing and playing these two chords, play the strumming patterns below.

First pattern: Count and tap ONE-TWO-THREE-FOUR along with your metronome. Then strum downward at *each* click. Remember each strum must be struck exactly on each sound of count. Sustain fully for one count without making the sound of the chord too short or too long.

Second pattern: Count ONE-TWO-THREE-FOUR, strum at ONE, sustain it for two counts, then strike again at THREE and at FOUR.

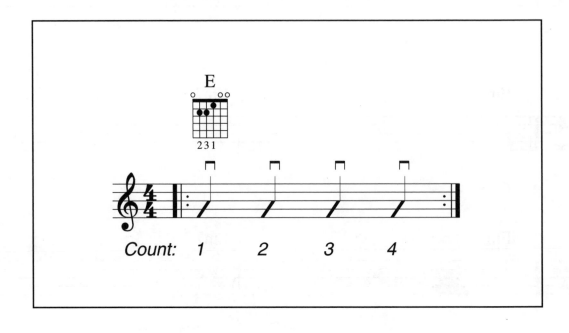

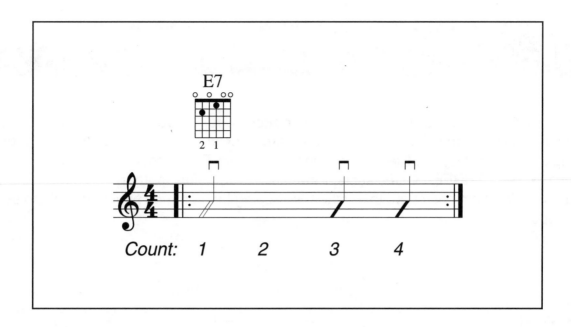

Now try the exercises below and practice the two strumming patterns and connecting the E and E7 chords. Remember *not to* move your common fingers, 1st and 2nd. Just lift your 3rd finger when moving from E to E7 and press it down when moving from E7 to E.

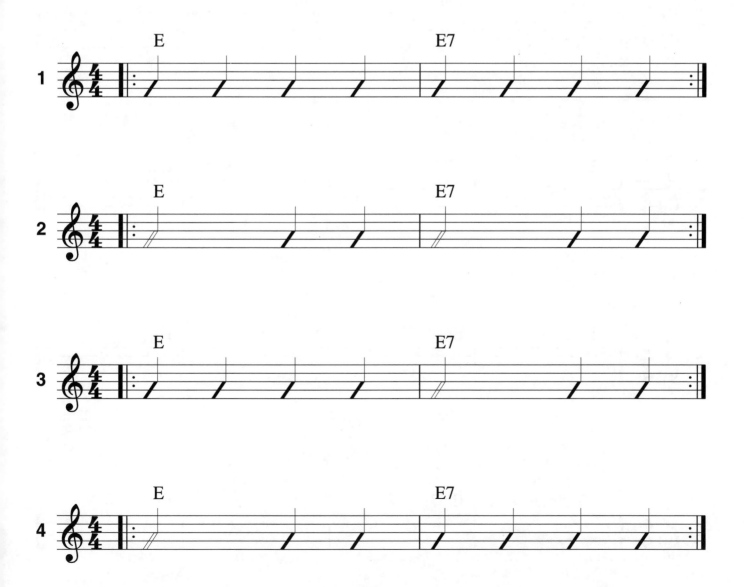

REVIEW 1

Review all the chords and the strumming patterns you have learned so far. Then pick a strumming pattern and play it through each exercise or write out several patterns of your choice, combining them in any way you like as shown in the example. Remember to use a metronome, count and tap ONE-TWO-THREE-FOUR, sustain the slashes fully for appropriate counts, and make a smooth connection from one chord to another by keeping the common fingers down and by moving only the necessary fingers.

Ex:

Em   Em7   Em   E

1

Em   Em7   Em   E

2

E   E7   E   Em

3

Em7   Em   E   E7

4

E7   Em7   E   Em

2-3

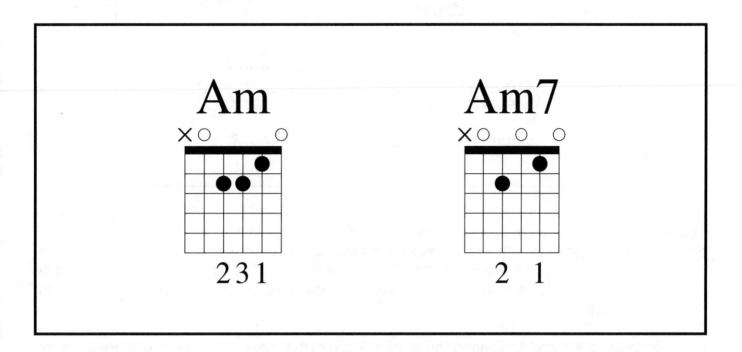

This section introduces two chords, Am and Am7. Notice the similarities between Am and E, and Am7 and E7. They have exactly the same shapes! The only difference in both cases is that the hand has shifted to a different place. Press E, hold the shape as you lift it off, and then move it *a string downward* so that your 2nd finger will be on the 4th string instead of the 5th string. You now have Am. Do the same for Am7: press E7, lift it off, keep your hand in the same shape and shift it one string down. Note that there is an X mark on the 6th string for both chords. As you may recall, X means the string is not to be played.

Once you feel comfortable with pressing these two chords, play the two new strumming patterns shown. Notice the patterns include an eighth note slash which gets 1/2 count; there are two eighth note slashes in ONE count or click; one quarter note slash is equal to two eighth note slashes. To get an eighth note feeling, think of dividing a quarter note exactly by half and then count **ONE-*and*-TWO-*and*-THREE-*and*-FOUR-*and***. When tapping your foot, tap down on ONE, then tap up on *and*. Similarly, foot down on TWO and up on *and*, down on THREE and up on *and*, etc.

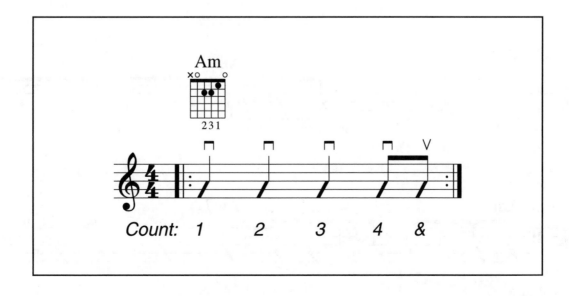

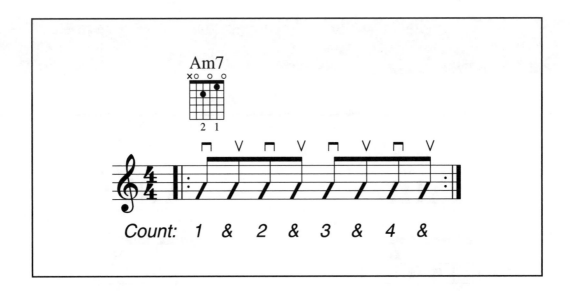

The upstroke, V, is played by brushing one or more of the strings, in this case with the Am and Am7 chords, from the 1st to the 5th strings towards the ceiling. Relax your wrist and practice down-up, down-up until you get used to the movement. Play downstrokes right on each click and upstrokes on *ands* as shown in the strumming pattern for Am7. Play them repeatedly until you can play without dragging or rushing.

When connecting Am and Am7, apply the same rules from the previous sections; keep the common fingers down and move only the fingers necessary to play the next chord. In this case, keep the 1st and 2nd fingers down and press or lift off the 3rd finger only.

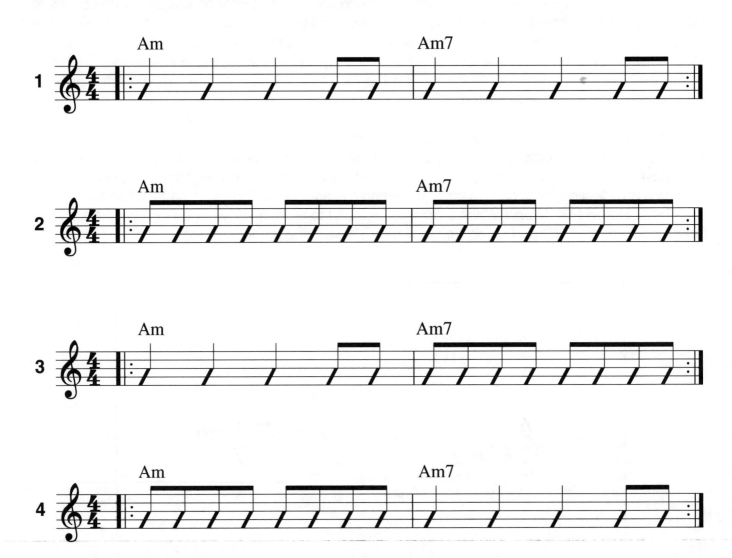

2-4

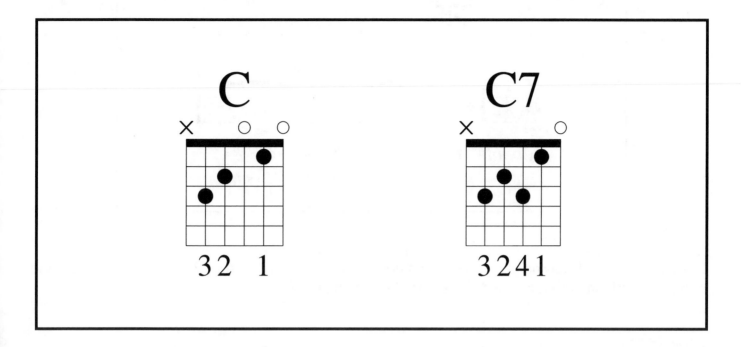

C and C7 are the new chords here. You may find it a little hard to play the C chord without touching the neighboring strings at first. Practice until you can hear each string and note clearly without any buzz. (If you have some difficulties holding these chords, place a capo at the 2nd or 3rd fret.)

You may notice that the C chord can be played simply by first pressing Am7 and then adding a note on the 5th string, 3rd fret with your 3rd finger.

In order to play C7 from C, all you need to do is to add your 4th finger on the 3rd fret of the 3rd string. When you can play these two chords at ease, try the following strumming patterns which combine some of the rhythms you have already seen.

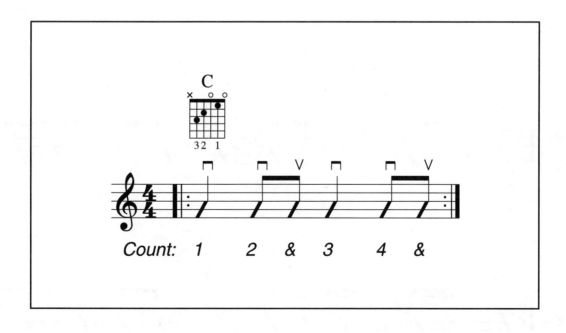

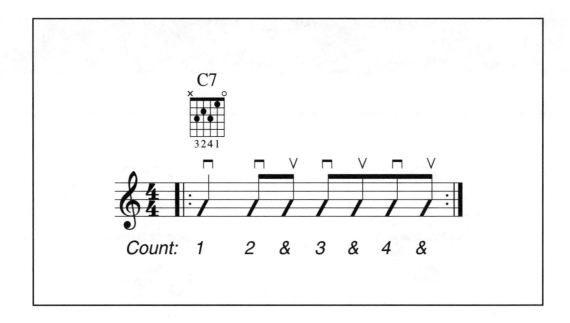

Now, practice the following exercises. When connecting between C and C7, keep the common fingers, 1st, 2nd, and 3rd down and move only the 4th finger.

REVIEW 2

Review each chord and strumming pattern you have learned so far. Play a pattern of your choice through the progression or combine several patterns in any way you like as shown in the example. Make sure to use a metronome, count and tap, sustain the slashes fully for appropriate counts, and make a smooth connection from one chord to another by keeping the common fingers down and by moving only the necessary fingers. When moving from E to Am or from E7 to Am7 in #4, lift off all your fingers, *keep* the same chord shape, and shift it to a string downward. Practice the movement slowly and repeatedly until it becomes a smooth transition.

Ex:

1

C   Am7   C   Am7

2

C   Am   C   Am

3

C7   C   Am   C

4

E   Am   E7   Am7

NAMING A CHORD

A chord is named after the bottom note called the *root*. The root is the principal note on which a chord is built. The E chord is called *E* because its root is the E note as played by an open 6th string. Am is called *Am* because it is a minor chord built upon the note A or an open 5th string. To be able to connect between the shape of the open chords and their names, it is essential that you know the name of the notes of the guitar in open position. On the next page, you will see a diagram illustrating this. You do not have to memorize all the notes and their locations right now, but come back to the diagram whenever you learn a new open chord and locate its root so that you will better grasp the origin of the chord name.

Examples:

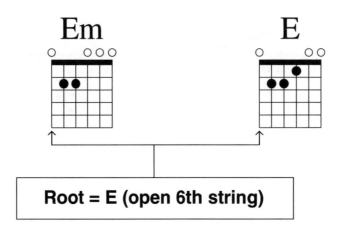

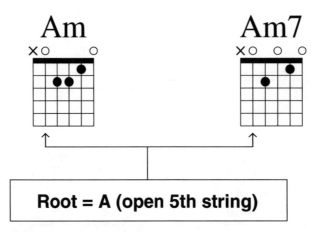

NOTES IN THE OPEN POSITION

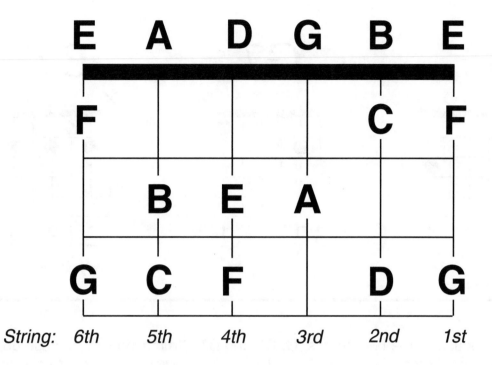

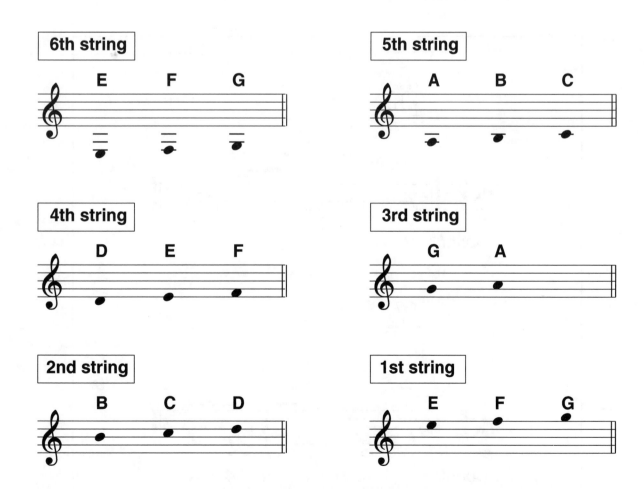

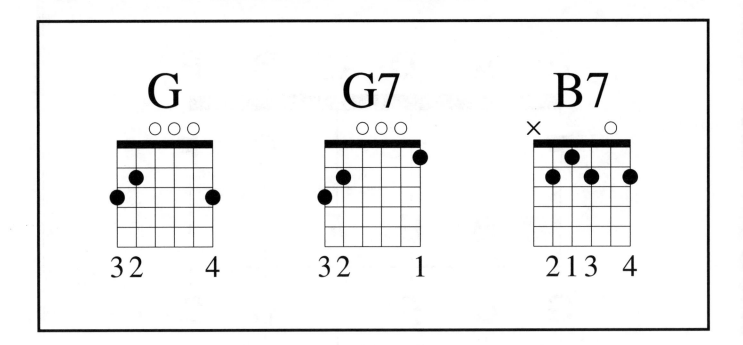

This section introduces three new chords, G, G7 and B7. Strumming patterns use quarter and eighth note slashes in combinations different from the previous sections. Notice the accent symbol, >, which tells you to put a stronger emphasis on notes or slashes.

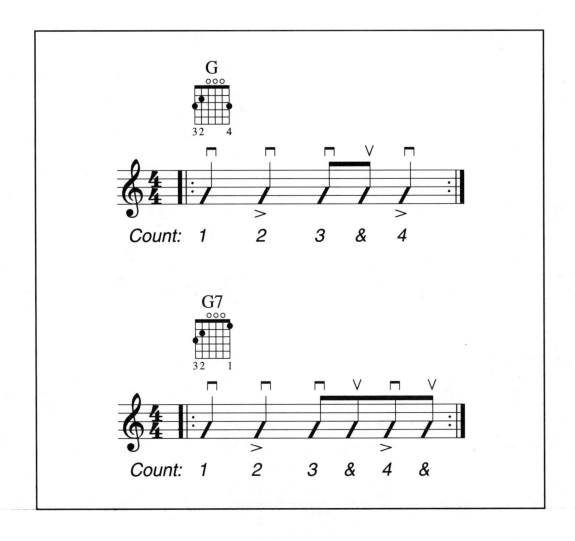

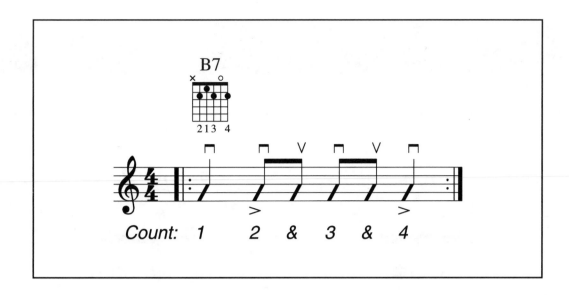

When moving from G to B7, keep the 2nd finger on the 5th string, slide down your 4th finger on the 1st string from the 3rd fret to the 2nd fret instead of lifting it off, and press your 1st and 3rd fingers on the 4th and the 3rd strings respectively. (You may notice that although it does not move to another fret or lift off, the 2nd finger will naturally adjust its position slightly by sliding down a little within the 2nd fret.) Practice this movement over and over without strumming at first until you can do the transition smoothly without looking at the guitar.

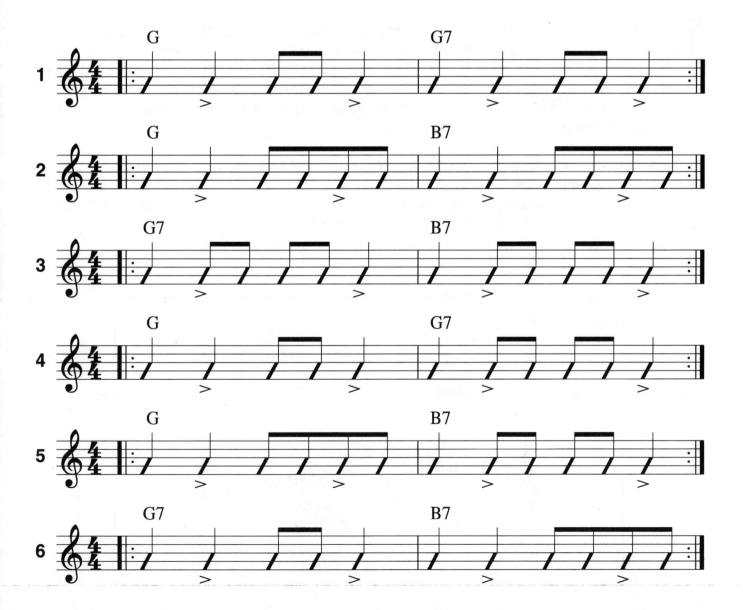

2-6

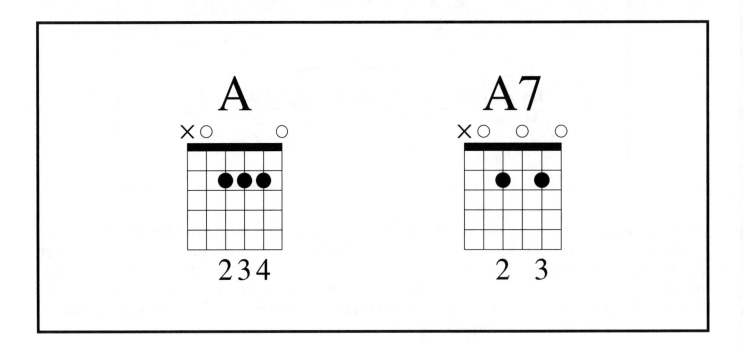

This section introduces a *tie*, ⌣ , in the strumming patterns. A tie indicates that the chord is to be sounded or attacked only once and held for the time value of both slashes combined. For instance, the first strumming pattern *ties* the eighth-note slash at the *and* of the 2nd beat and the half-note slash at the 3rd beat. In this case, you play a chord at *and of the 2nd* and hold it for 2 1/2 beats—or the total time values of both slashes. Count loudly and make sure to sustain fully for correct time values for each pattern.

If your fingers keep touching the neighboring strings when playing the A chord, remember to keep the three fingers tightly *together* and straight. As for the fingerings, some players alternatively use their 1st, 2nd, and 3rd fingers to press the A chord, instead of 2nd, 3rd, and 4th fingers as shown here. You can also use your 1st and 2nd fingers to finger A7.

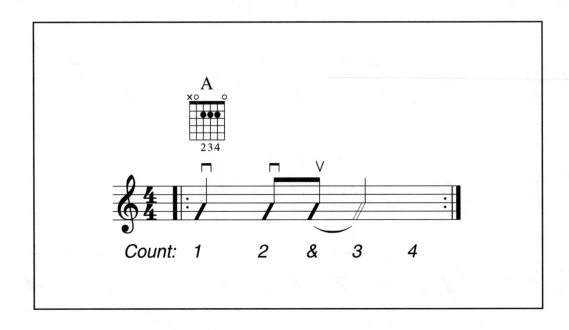

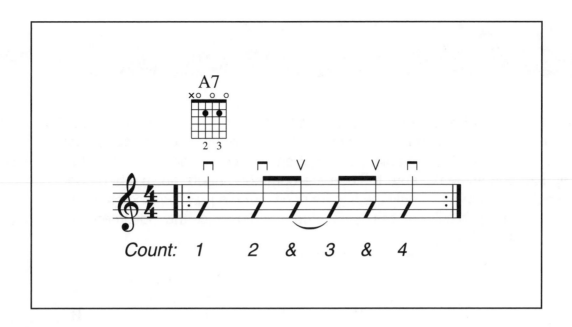

When moving from A to A7, keep your 2nd finger down and move your 3rd finger from the 3rd to the 2nd string while lifting your 4th finger off.

REVIEW 3

Review each chord and the strumming patterns you have learned so far. Play a particular strumming pattern throughout or write out the patterns of your choice, combining them in any way you like as shown in the example. Use a metronome, count and tap, and sustain the slashes fully for appropriate counts. Make sure to keep the common fingers down when connecting from one chord to another and to move only the fingers necessary to play the next chord. If you have trouble connecting in some particular places, isolate them and practice the movement *very* slowly.

Ex:

1

2

3

4

2-7

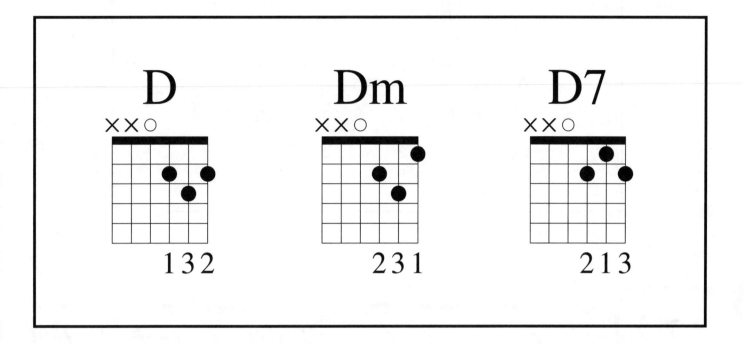

Study the chord diagrams carefully and follow the fingerings. Notice the X marks on the 6th and 5th strings which are not to be played when strumming.

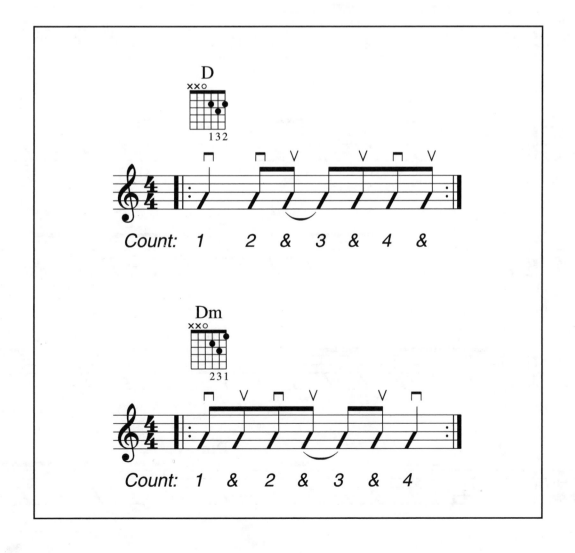

42

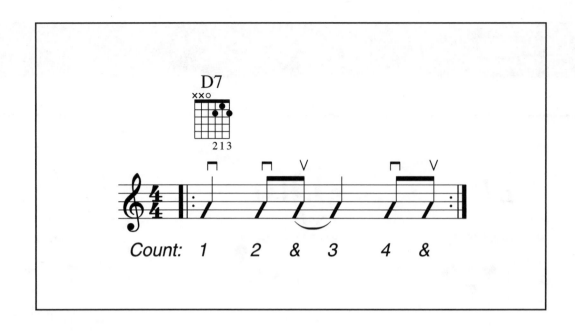

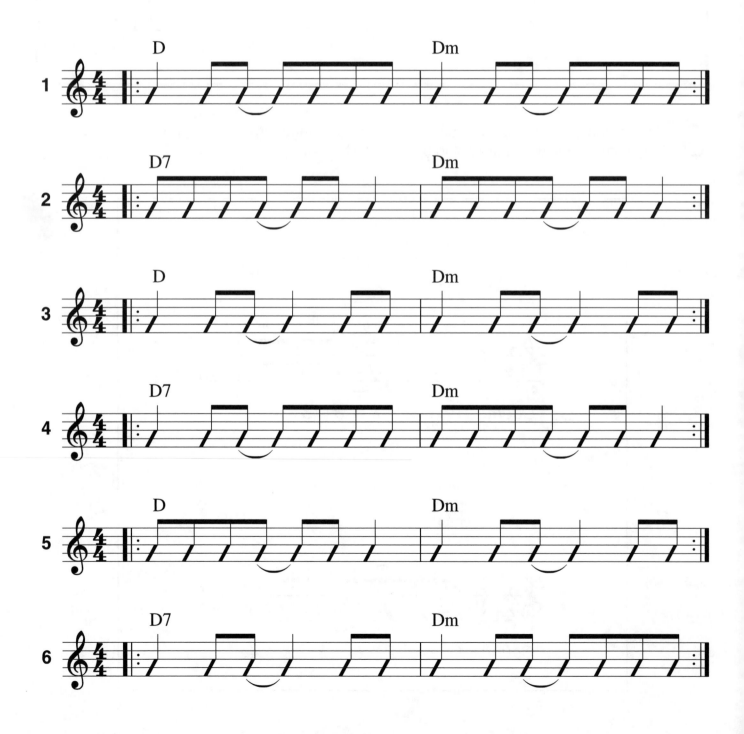

2-8

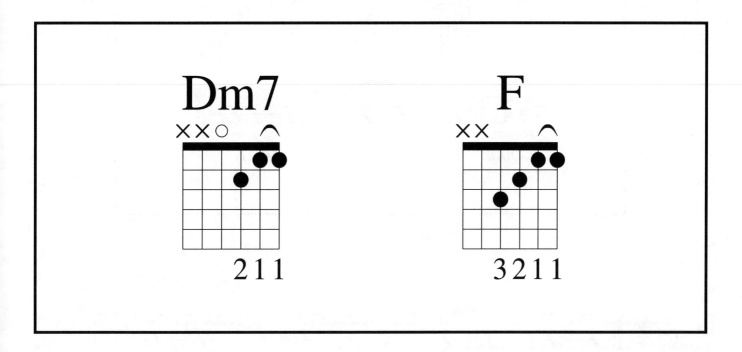

The two new chords, Dm7 and F, are played by the use of the *barre* technique. The technique consists of covering two or more strings using the flat part of a finger, in this case the 1st finger while keeping your thumb behind the neck.

In order to play Dm7, first barre the 1st and 2nd strings at the 1st fret using your 1st finger, then place the tip of the 2nd finger on the 2nd fret of the 3rd string. F can be played by adding the 3rd finger on the 3rd fret of the 4th string while holding Dm7.

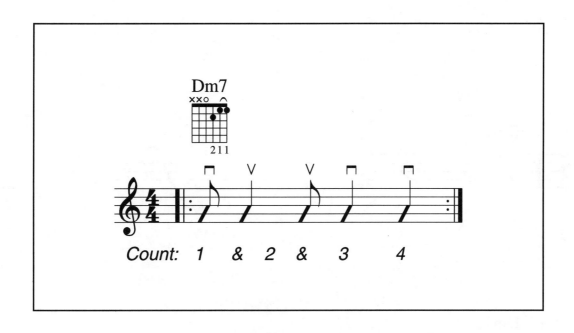

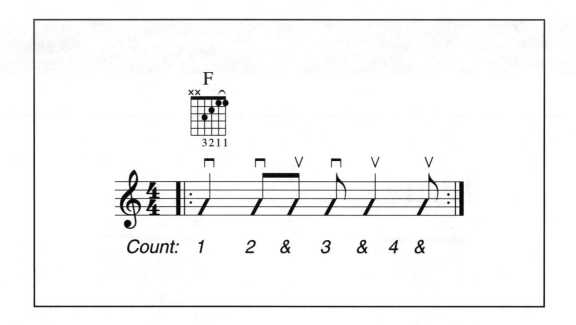

REVIEW 4

Review each chord and the strumming patterns you have learned so far. Take one pattern and play it throughout or write down and play several patterns of your choice, combining them in any way you like as shown in the example. Use a metronome, count and tap, and sustain the slashes fully for appropriate counts. Keep the common fingers down when connecting from one chord to another and move only the fingers necessary to play the next chord whenever possible. Sometimes, you do not always have common fingers or find the same shape of the chords such as in the movements from C to G in #5 and from D7 to G in #6 in the repeat. In these cases, after playing the first chord, lift off all fingers together and then simply finger the next chord. *Visualizing* the shape of the next chord in your mind often helps you to make a smooth connection. Practice the movement *very slowly* at first connecting to different chords.

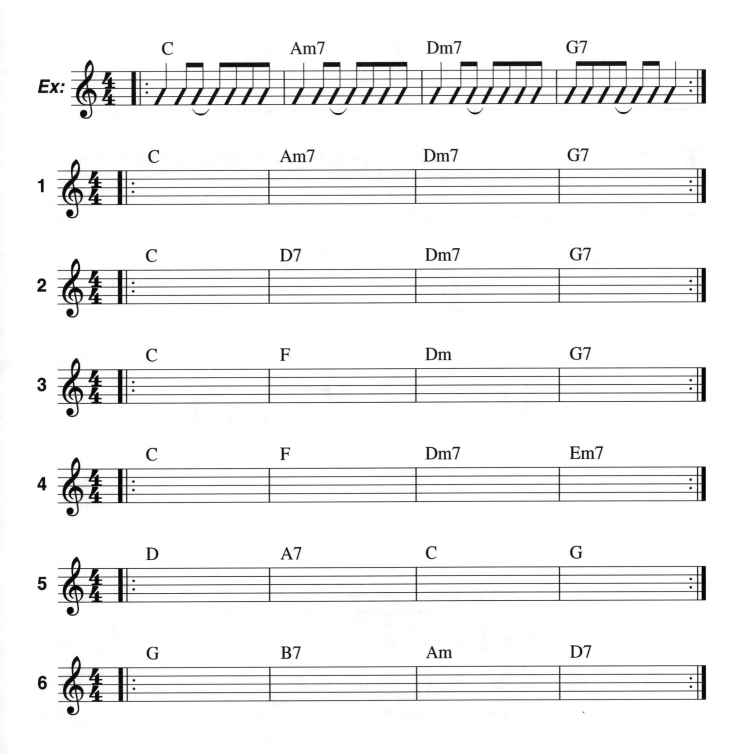

2-9

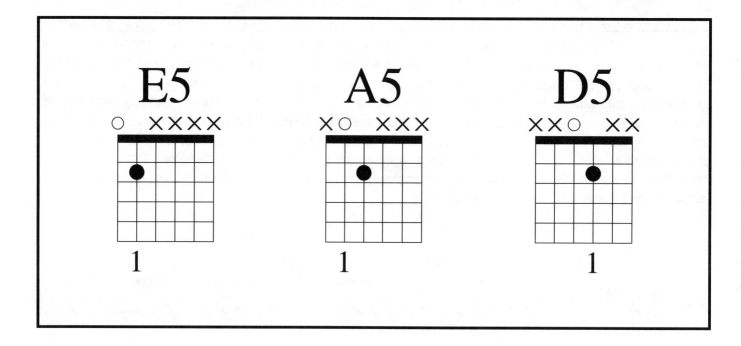

The so-called *power chords* are introduced here. The power chords are the foundation of many blues, rock and heavy-metal songs and they are perfect for hard-driving rhythm guitar parts. Fingerings are not difficult, but note the X marks where strings are not to be played. Typically, they are played with consecutive downstrokes brushing only two strings as indicated in each pattern.

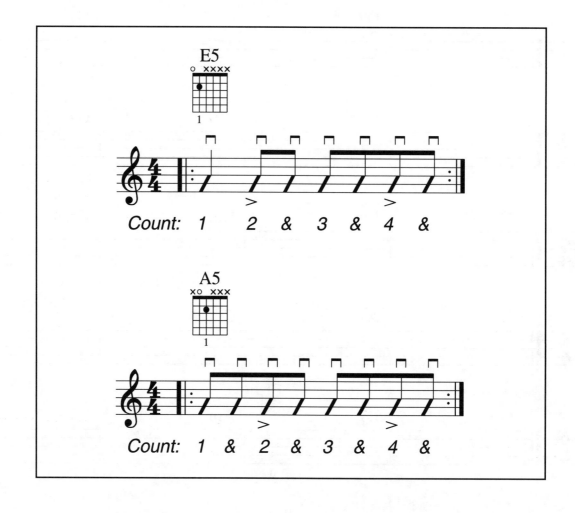

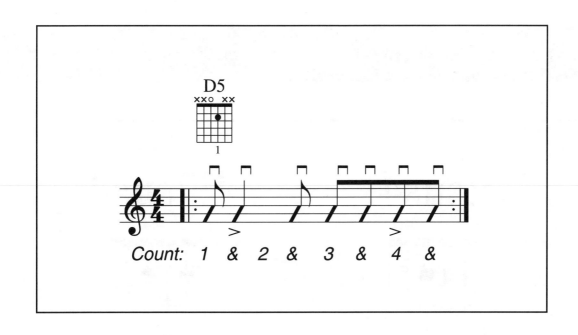

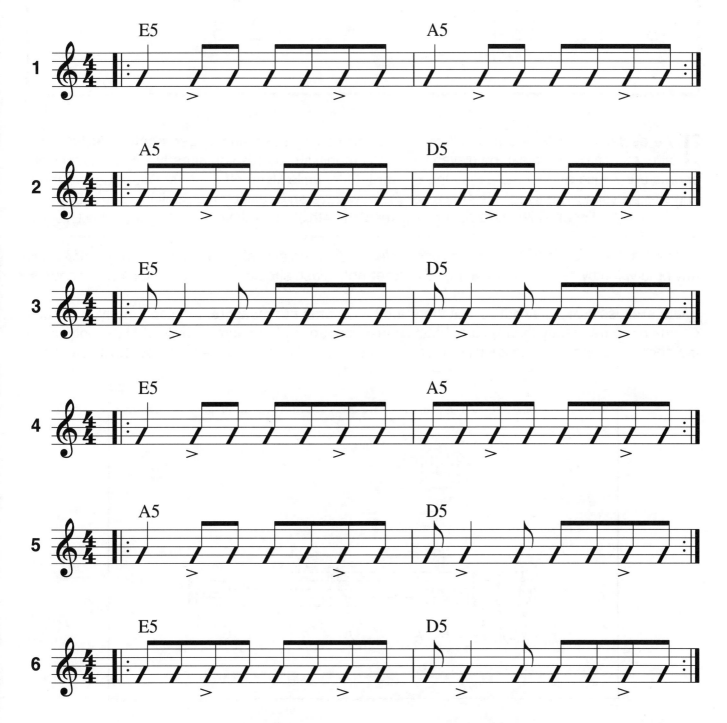

2-10

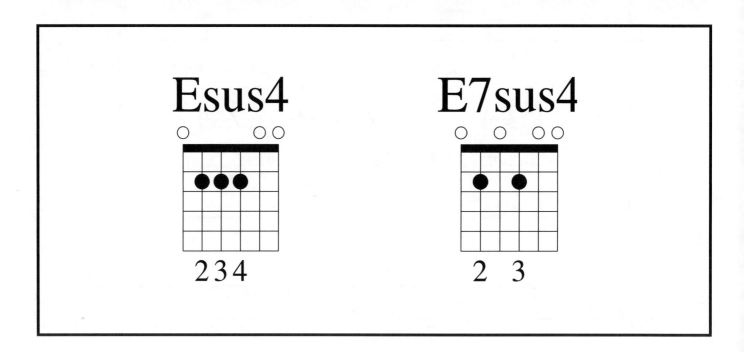

Esus4   E7sus4

The sections *2-10* through *2-13* will introduce you to *sus4* and *7sus4* chords. As you will see, each new chord can be played by slightly modifying chords you already know. The first two chords are Esus4 and E7sus4. Play the E chord, then while lifting off your 1st finger, use your 4th finger to press the 2nd fret of the 4th string. You now have an Esus4 chord. Similarly, finger E7, then remove the 1st finger while pressing the 2nd fret of the 4th string with your 3rd finger to play E7sus4.

Notice that the strumming patterns include dotted quarter-note slashes. If you recall, a *dot* increases any note value by half, therefore a dotted quarter-note slash should be sustained for 1 & 1/2 counts.

In the exercises, you may notice that there are two chords per measure, requiring that you change chords more frequently than before. Practice just connecting the chords slowly at first—only move the necessary fingers while keeping to press the common fingers down—then add the strumming.

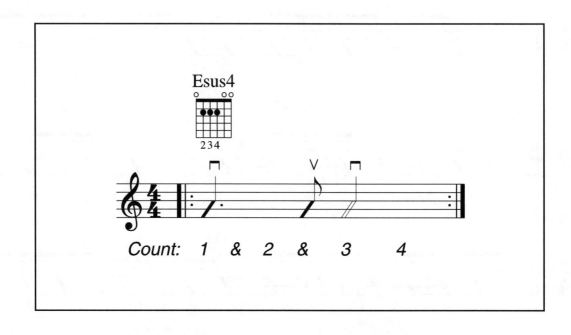

Esus4

Count: 1   &   2   &   3   4

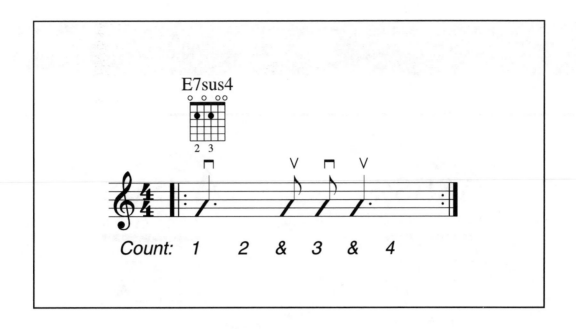

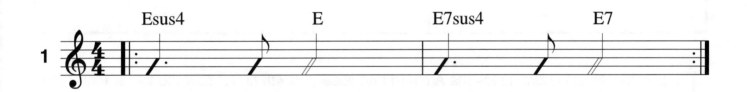

1

2

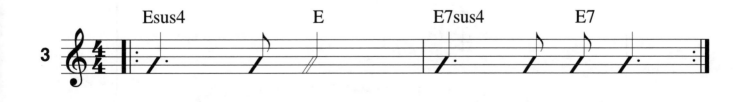

3

4

2-11

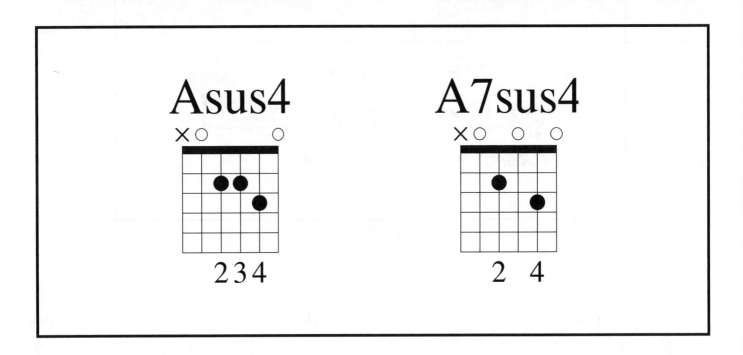

To play the Asus4 chord, press the A chord and slide your 4th finger down to the 3rd fret of the 2nd string. Similarly, to play A7sus4, press A7 first, then remove your 3rd finger while pressing the 3rd fret of the 2nd string with your 4th finger.

Notice that each strumming pattern includes a tie. Count carefully and sustain fully for correct time values.

In the exercises, there are again two chords per measure, but notice where the second chord is placed; it is on *and* of the 2nd beat.

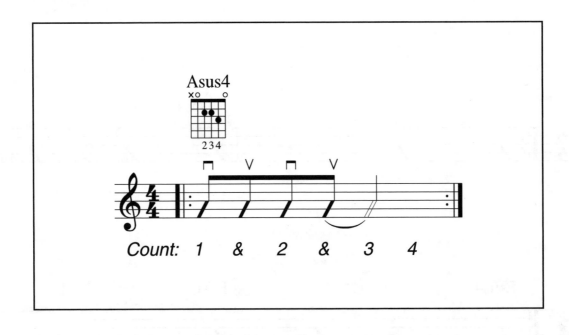

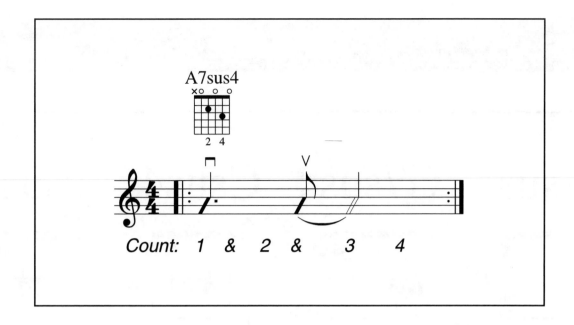

Count: 1 & 2 & 3 4

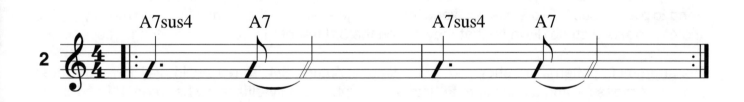

1

2

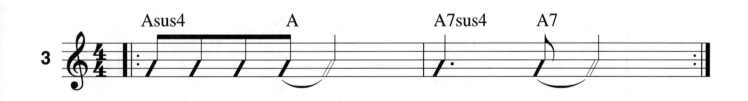

3

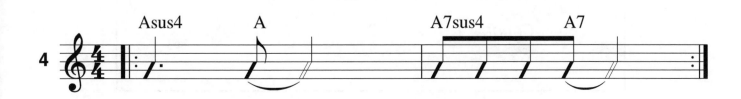

4

2-12

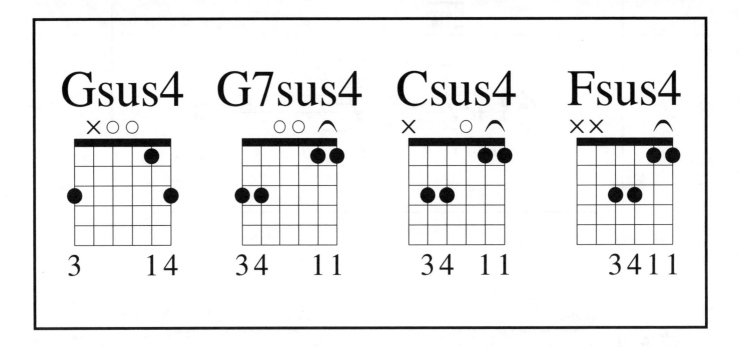

You may need to stretch your hand a little to play a Gsus4 chord. Play G, lift off your 2nd finger and add the 1st finger on the 1st fret of the 2nd string. You can mute the X-marked 5th string by tilting your 3rd finger and lightly touching the string so that no sound will be heard even if you strum the string. G7sus4, Csus4, and Fsus4 have very similar chord shapes and exactly the same fingerings. All use the 1st finger barring the 1st and 2nd strings respectively. While keeping the barre, press your 3rd finger on the 3rd fret of the 6th string and 4th finger on the 3rd fret of the 5th string to play G7sus4. To play Csus4, keep the 1st finger-barre on the same place and move your 3rd and 4th fingers a string down so that they are on the 3rd fret of the 5th and 4th strings respectively.

The strumming patterns are shown in a new time signature, 3/4. To review, in 3/4, there are three beats in a measure and a quarter note gets one count. The only difference between 4/4 and 3/4 is the number of counts in a measure; the rest is the same.

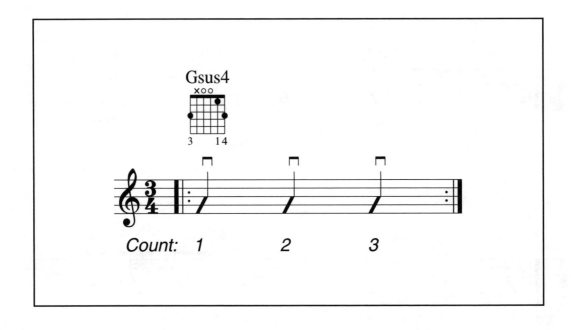

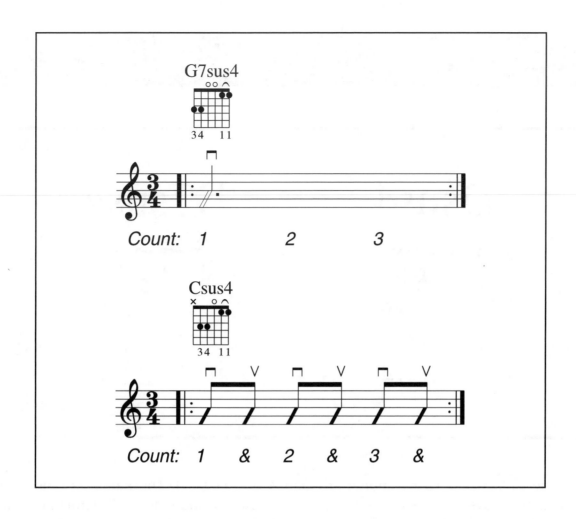

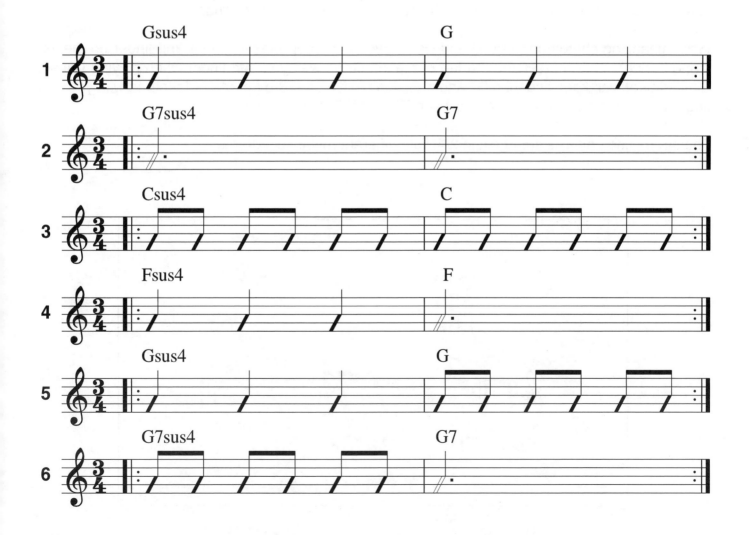

2-13

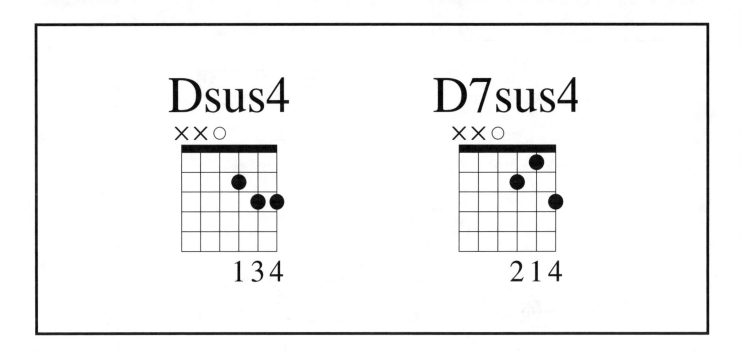

The last two sus4 and 7sus4 chords are Dsus4 and D7sus4. The same as before, press D chord, then remove your 2nd finger while placing your 4th finger on the 3rd fret of the 1st string. You now have Dsus4. Similarly, play D7, lift off your 3rd finger and then place your 4th finger on the same place as in Dsus4, the 3rd fret of the 1st string. D7sus4 is in your hand.

When changing chords between D and Dsus4, you can keep pressing your 2nd finger on the 1st string throughout and press the 3rd fret of the 1st string with your 4th finger when playing Dsus4. Similarly, you can keep fingering D7 and press on or lift off the 3rd fret of the 1st string with your 4th finger during the chord connection between D7 and D7sus4.

The strumming patterns are again in 3/4, with different rhythmic patterns.

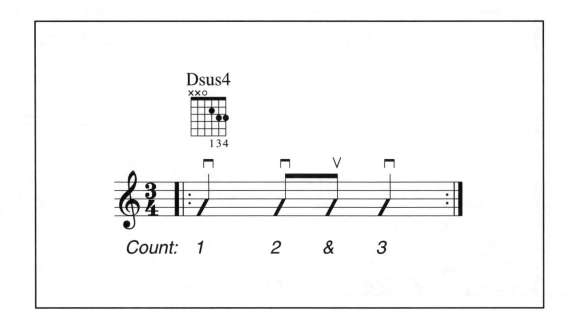

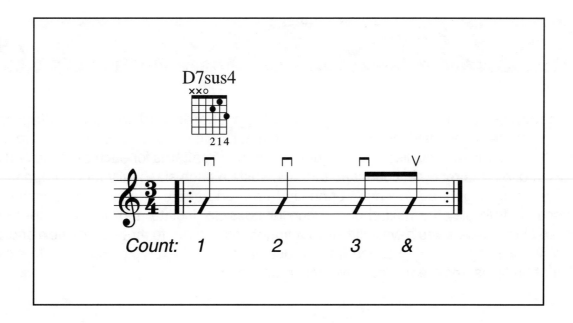

CHAPTER 2 REVIEW

This section is a Chapter review. Review all the chords and the strumming patterns. Choose a pattern and play each exercise through. Or write out several patterns of your choice, combining them in any way you like. Practice both 4/4 and 3/4 patterns for each exercise and remember *always* to use a metronome, count and tap, and sustain each slash fully for appropriate counts. Keep the common fingers down when connecting from one chord to another and move only the fingers necessary to play the next chord whenever possible. Isolate and practice repeatedly and *slowly* those places where you have to lift all your fingers off in order to move to the next chord. At the end, you'll find a song, *Amazing Grace* with an accompaniment example. Feel free to experiment with different patterns and create your own accompaniment.

1

| C | Dm7 | G7sus4 | G7 | C |

2

| A | Asus4 | Esus4 | E | A |

3

| C7 | F | A7 | Dm | Dm |

4

| A5 | D5 | A5 | E5 | A5 |

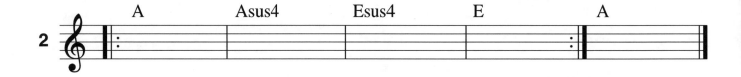

5

| D5 | A5 | E5 | A5 | A5 |

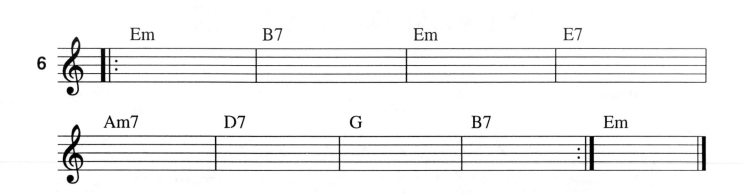

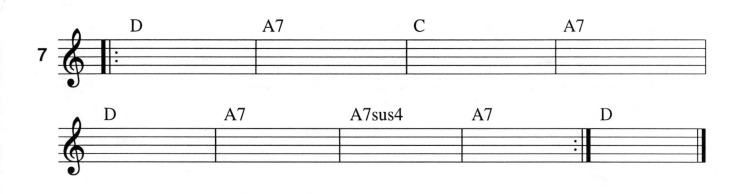

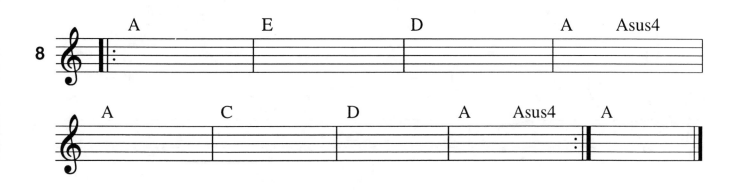

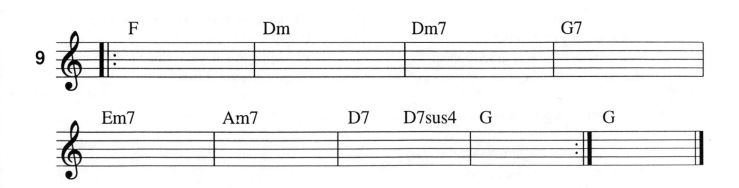

AMAZING GRACE

Adagio

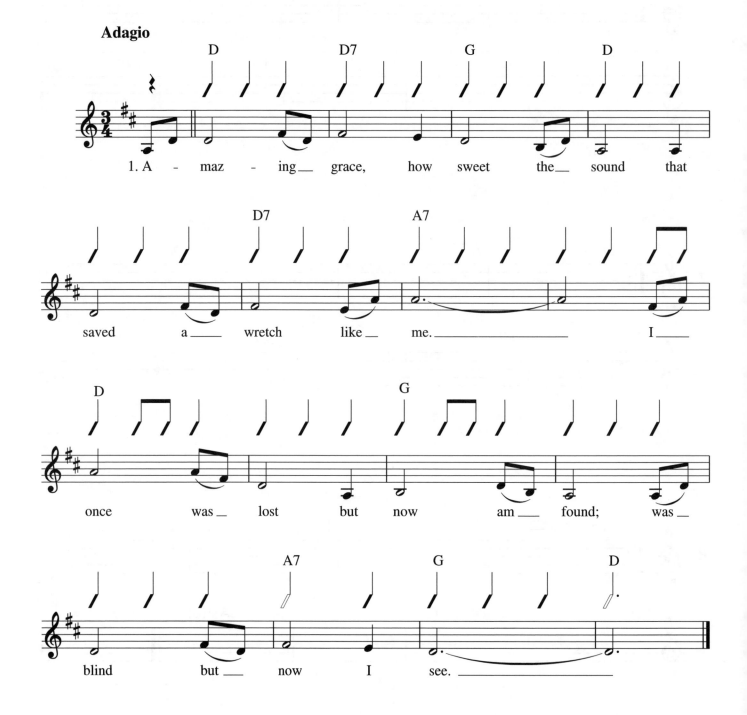

Additional Lyrics

2. 'Twas grace that taught my heart to fear,
   And grace my fears relieved,
   How precious did that grace appear
   The hour I first believed.

3. Thru many dangers, toils and snares
   I have already come.
   'Tis grace has brought me safe thus far,
   And grace will lead me home.

4. When we've been there ten thousand years,
   Bright shining as the sun.
   We've no less days to sing God's praise
   Than when we'd first begun.

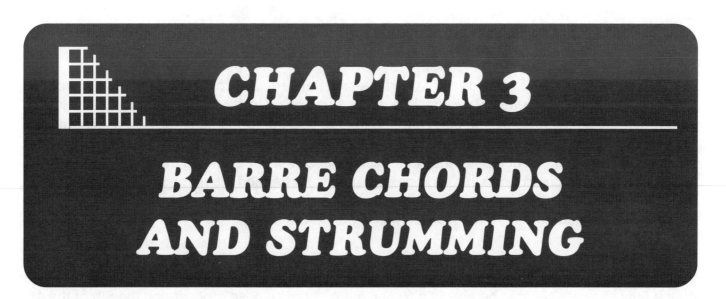

CHAPTER 3
BARRE CHORDS AND STRUMMING

WHAT IS A BARRE CHORD?

A *barre chord* takes its name from the role of the 1st finger of your left hand. This finger acts as a *bar* across the fingerboard, depressing all six strings and replacing the nut (the ivory piece at the top of the neck). By using your 1st finger as a bar, you can move many of the open chords you have learned up and down on the fingerboard.

To understand this, first grab your guitar and play an E chord as shown below. Note in order for the 1st finger to be used as a barre, the fingering has to be changed slightly; use your 2nd, 3rd and 4th fingers instead of the usual 1st, 2nd and 3rd fingers. Now move the chord up one fret and lay your 1st finger across the 1st fret, covering all six strings. You are now holding your first barre chord, F.

The new barred F chord is essentially the same as the F chord you have learned in *2-8*, only the 1st finger barres *all* six strings instead of just the 1st and 2nd strings. In the same manner, move this F chord up two frets, 1st finger barring the 3rd fret and maintaining the E chord shape. You now have an alternative way to play an G chord. Moving the same chord shape further up two frets will produce an A chord.

E CHORD	F CHORD
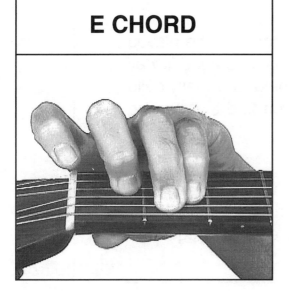	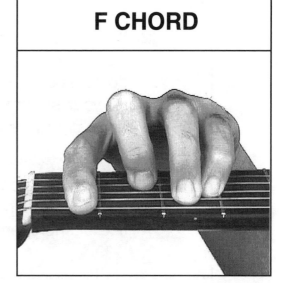

NAME OF THE BARRE CHORDS

As you have seen, the open chords are named after the name of their roots. An E chord has a root on the 6th string, open; when you play a simple open E, it was noted in the section "NAMING A CHORD" (p. 34) that the 6th string is played open and the bottom E is the root note of the chord. Likewise, all the barre chords in the shape of an E chord have roots on the 6th string and they are all named after the notes of the 6th string at the fret that your 1st finger barres. For example, the chord up one fret E chord is called an *F* chord since the 1st finger lies on the 1st fret and the name of the note on the 1st fret of the 6th string is *F*. Similarly, if you play the same chord shape at the 5th fret, it is named a *A* chord because you barre the 5th fret which has *A* on the 6th string.

In order to be able to utilize the E-shaped barre chords anywhere on the neck, you need to know all the names of the notes on the 6th string. Likewise, you have to be aware of the names of the notes on the 5th or the 4th string to be able to play any barre chords whose roots are on the 5th or the 4th string. Do not feel overwhelmed by this! Nobody is able to memorize all the notes overnight. Take your time and learn these notes gradually. Follow and practice the following sections every day and you will be able to recognize each note on each string before you know it.

In the following sections, you will see two basic forms of the barre chords: *E-form* and *A-form*. E-form chords have roots on the 6th string and A-form chords on the 5th string. Each form includes six barre chords which are based on six of the open chords you have already learned in the previous chapter. As mentioned, the purpose of this section is for you to learn the names of the notes on each string and to be able to move the barre chords anywhere on the fingerboard at ease. You will also learn some more strumming patterns.

SOME TIPS FOR PLAYING A BARRE CHORD

1. Keep your thumb behind the neck at all times. It should be directly opposite the 1st finger for maximum strength and effectiveness.

2. It often takes time until a barre chord can be played clearly without a buzz. Do not be discouraged if they do not sound perfect at the beginning. Gradually build up your strength and you will soon find that playing barre chords is no longer difficult.

3. Playing barre chords can become very tiring and puts a lot of pressure on your left hand and fingers. Practice for short periods at first and take breaks frequently.

E-FORM BARRE CHORDS

E-form barre chords have roots on the 6th string and they are all based on the open chords: **E, E7, Em, Em7, Esus4, E7sus4**.

NAMES OF THE NOTES ON THE 6TH STRING

Before we start, study the guitar fingerboard diagrams below and familiarize yourself with the location of the note on each fret of the 6th string. The names of the notes start with E, an open 6th string, then go up alphabetically: E, F, G, A, B, C, D, and so on. Note that at the 12th fret, E comes back and the same names repeat in the same order. The only difference is that those notes are an octave higher than the previous ones.

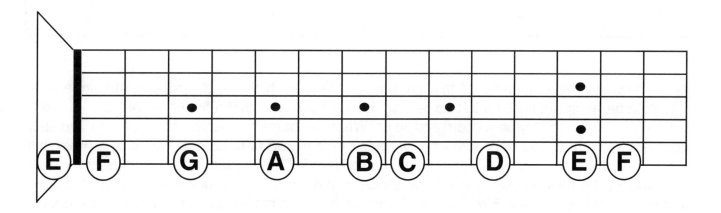

Each fret on the guitar represents a half-step. So between the notes on the above diagram, you have notes that are half a step higher or lower than them. Any note that is raised by a half-step is written with a symbol, ♯, called a *sharp*. Any note that is lowered by a half-step is written with a symbol, ♭, called a *flat*. For example, the note on the 2nd fret of the 6th string is called an F♯ (*F sharp*) because it is a half-step *higher* than an F. It can be also called a G♭ (*G flat*) as it is a half-step *lower* than a G. The notes in between the natural notes are shown below.

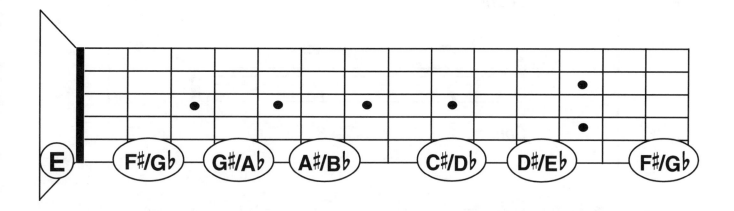

Go up and down and play each note, saying the names of the notes aloud. One of the effective ways to remember and recognize where the notes are is to use the position markers on the 3rd, 5th, 7th, 9th and 12th frets on your guitar. Memorize what note is on each fret on each position marker first, then learn and fill the other frets gradually.

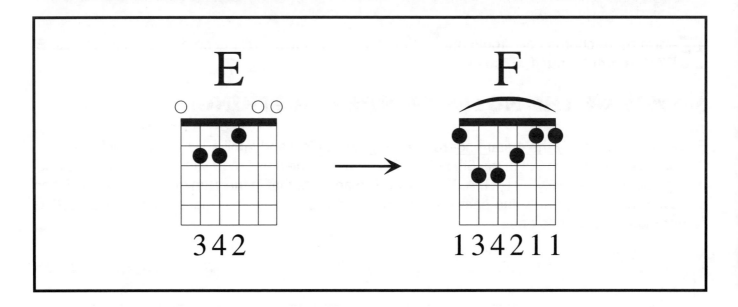

As shown at the beginning of this chapter, press E with the 2nd, 3rd and 4th fingers. To play a barre chord, shift it a fret up barring the 1st fret with your 1st finger to hold an F chord or shift it to the 5th fret to play an A chord and so on. Whatever barre chords you play, keep in mind each and every note should be clear without any notes being muted or buzzed. It may take a while until you can play a barre chord cleanly each time. Be patient and keep practicing. In the following exercises, you will be moving exactly the same shape of the chord up and down the fingerboard using different strumming patterns. First study and practice each strumming pattern using a simple open E chord.

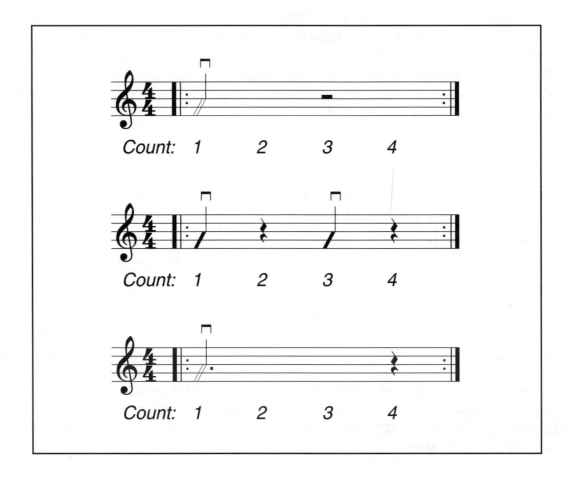

The rest after an open E chord or any other open chords should be muted by placing either your right hand or left hand lightly on the strings so that no sound will be heard. In case of a barre chord, all you need to do is release the pressure of your left hand so that the ringing of the chord will stop immediately. After you are comfortable with playing each pattern, try the following exercises with a metronome. Choose a pattern and play the exercise through as shown in #1, #2 and #3. Or write out several patterns of your choice combining in any way you like.

3-2

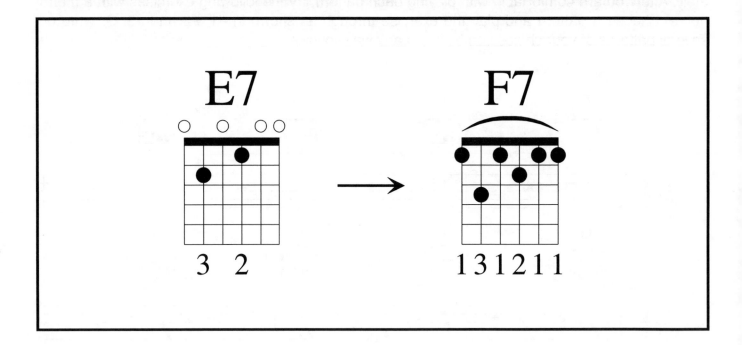

E7   F7

3 2   1 3 1 2 1 1

The barre chords in this section are based on E7. First, press E7 with your 3rd finger on the 2nd fret of the 5th string and the 2nd finger on the 1st fret of the 3rd string. Move this shape a fret up, barring all six strings at the 1st fret with your 1st finger to play F7. Shift this barre chord up and down the fingerboard as you have in the previous section. Two of the strumming patterns include some rests in places slightly different from before.

Count: 1   2   3   4

Count: 1   2   &   3   4   &

Count: 1   2   &   3   &   4

65

3-3

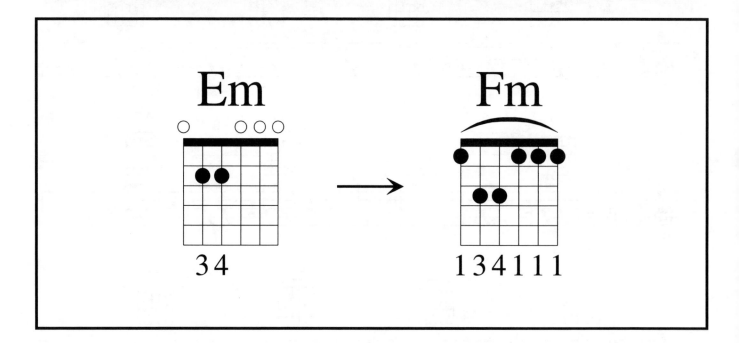

Em → Fm

3 4   1 3 4 1 1 1

Press Em with your 3rd finger on the 2nd fret of the 5th string and 4th finger on the 2nd fret of the 4th string. Keep the shape, shift a fret or two down and barre with your 1st finger. As many players do, you can place your 2nd finger above the 1st finger to enforce the barre. The X slashes on the strumming patterns indicate *mute*. When playing an open chord, you mute or deaden the strings by resting the palm of your right-hand while you continue strumming. In case of barre chords, use the same technique or lift your left hand slightly off the strings while brushing with down- or up-strokes.

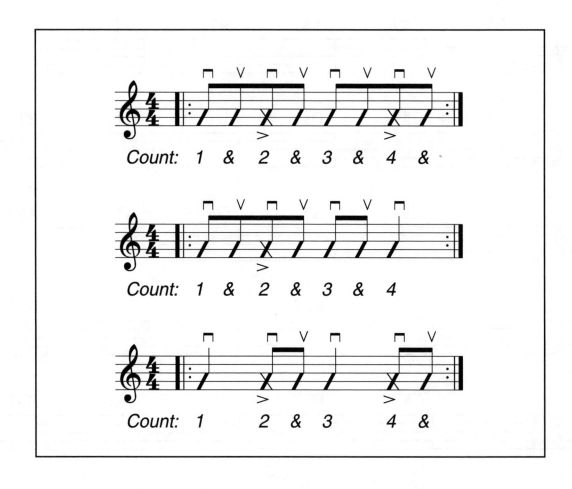

Count: 1 & 2 & 3 & 4 &

Count: 1 & 2 & 3 & 4

Count: 1   2 & 3   4 &

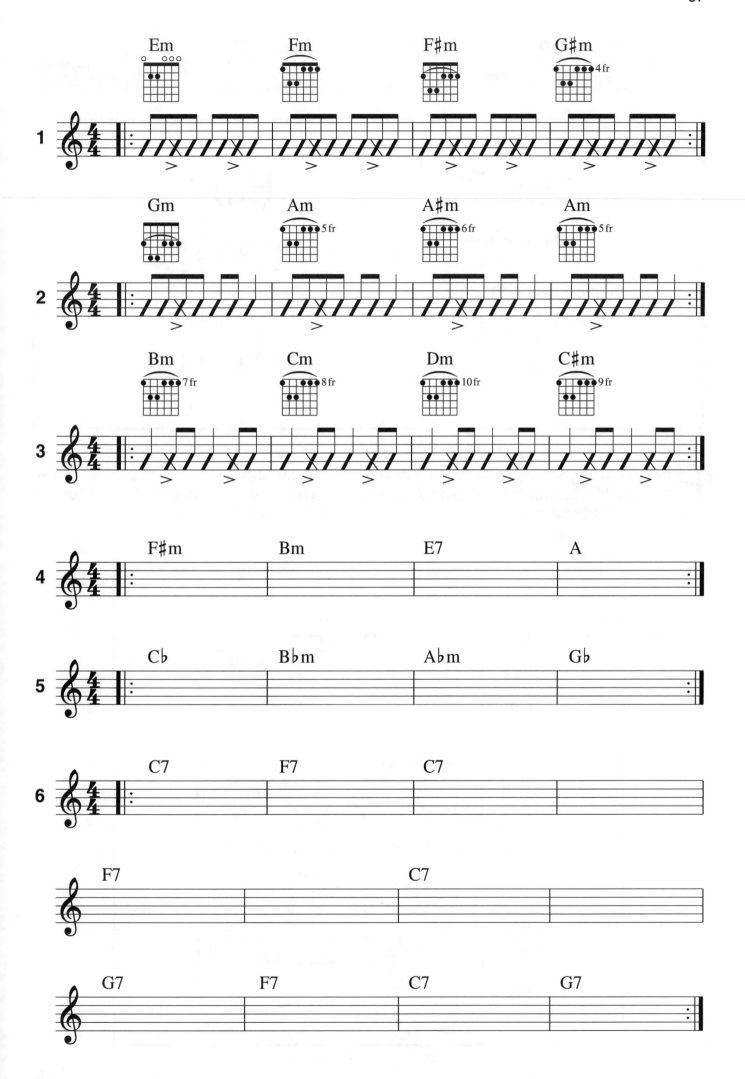

3-4

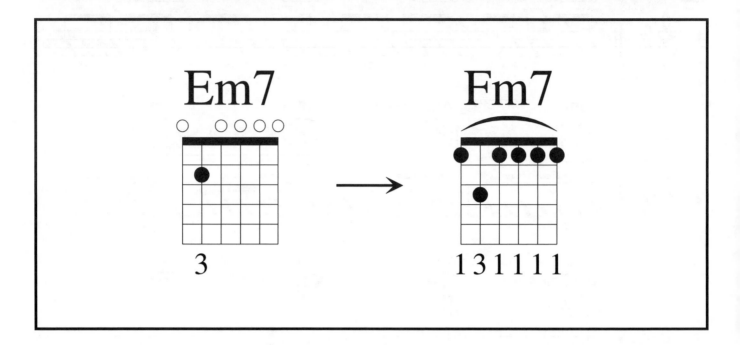

Em7   Fm7

3   1 3 1 1 1 1

Play Em7 with your 3rd finger instead of your 2nd finger. Shift it a fret or two up and barre the fret with your 1st finger. Again you can support your 1st-finger barre by placing your 2nd finger above it. The strumming patterns include muting with different rhythms.

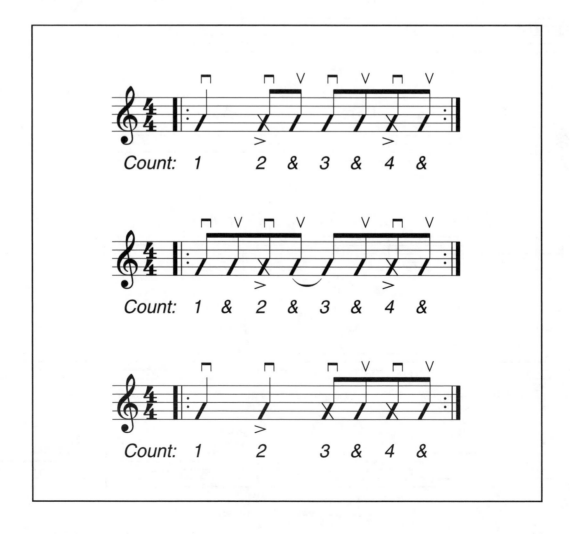

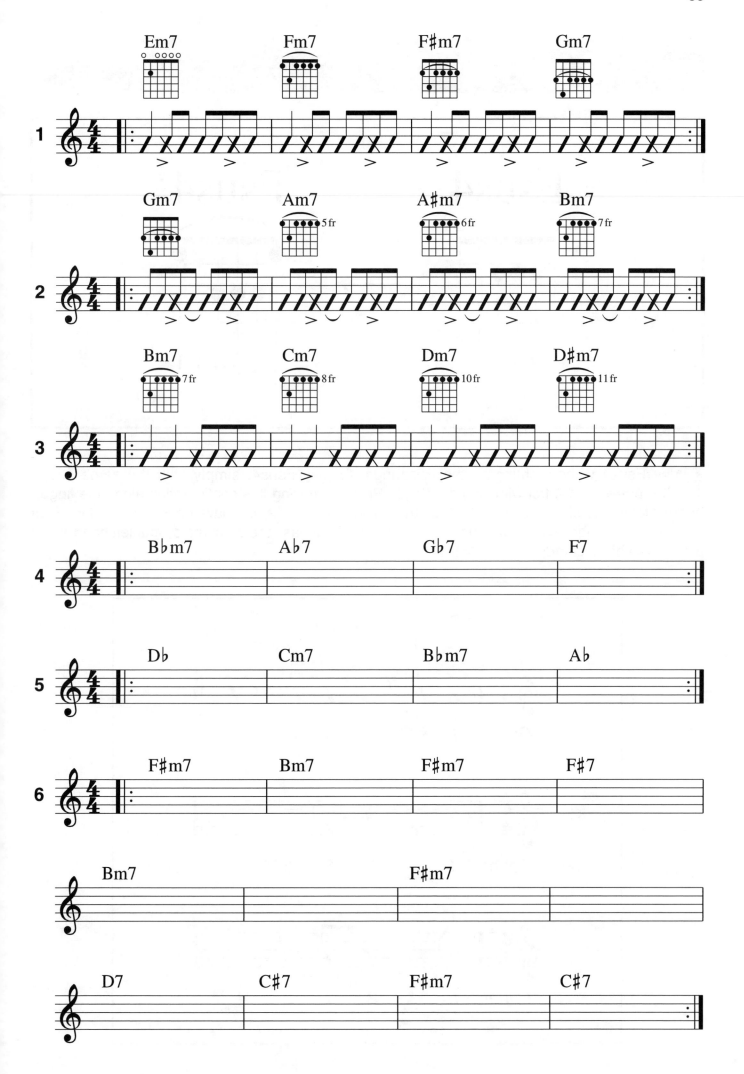

3-5

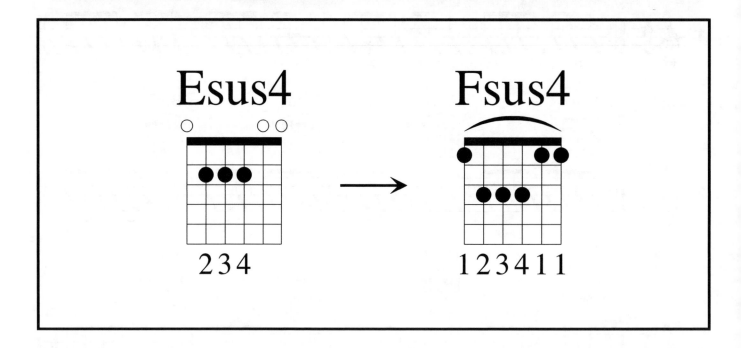

Esus4   →   Fsus4

P lay Esus4 without changing the fingerings. To play Fsus4, simply shift the same shape and barre the 1st fret with your 1st finger. Practice moving this configuration along the finger-board. Notice the eighth-note rest in the strumming patterns. As you have done before, place your right-hand palm lightly on the strings for open chords. Or release the pressure of your left hand when playing the barre chords.

Count: 1   &   2   &   3   &   4   &

Count: 1   &   2   &   3   4

Count: 1   &   2   &   3   4

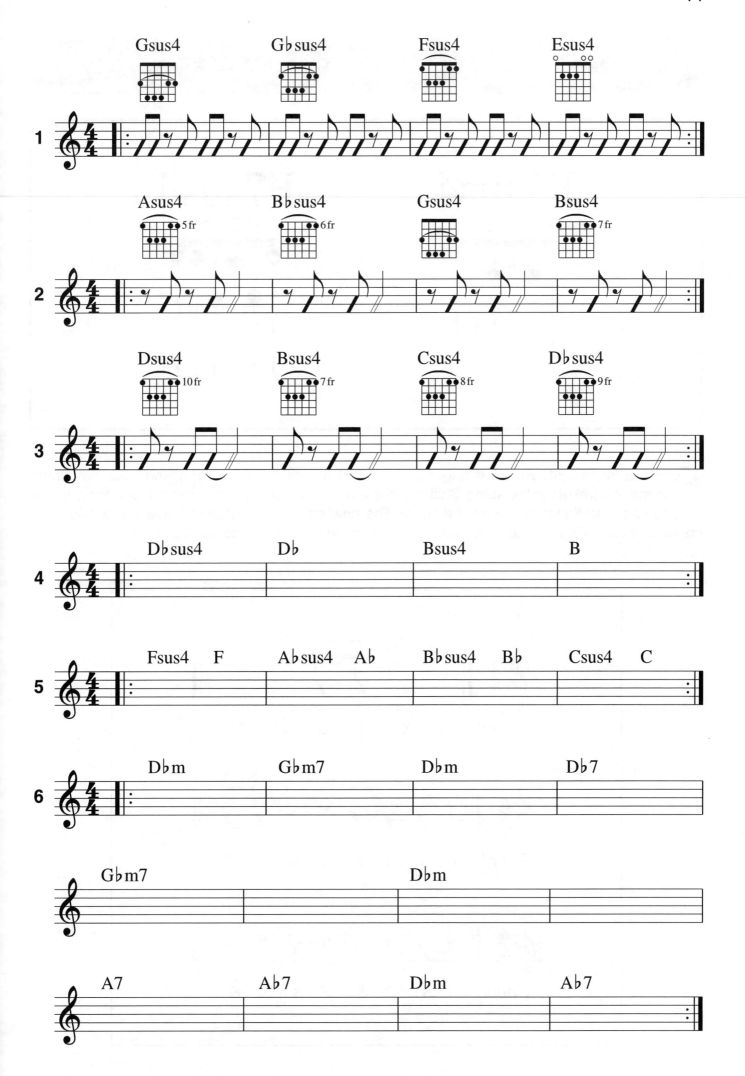

3-6

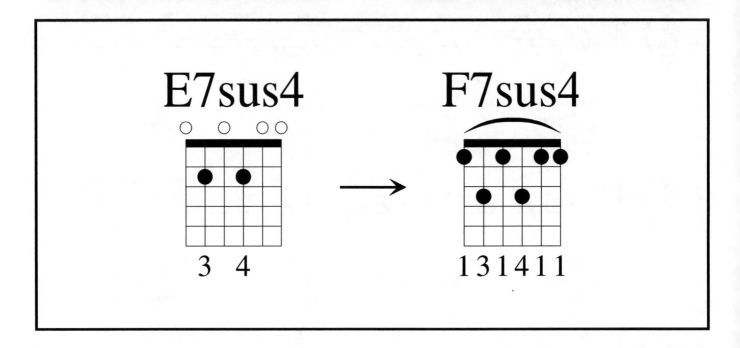

P ress E7sus4 with your 3rd finger on the 2nd fret of the 5th string and your 4th finger on the 2nd fret of the 3rd string. Shift and barre with your 1st finger. You can support the barre by placing your 2nd finger above the 1st finger. The new strumming patterns below are a little more complex. Take your time and make sure to slow it down to ensure a correct learning.

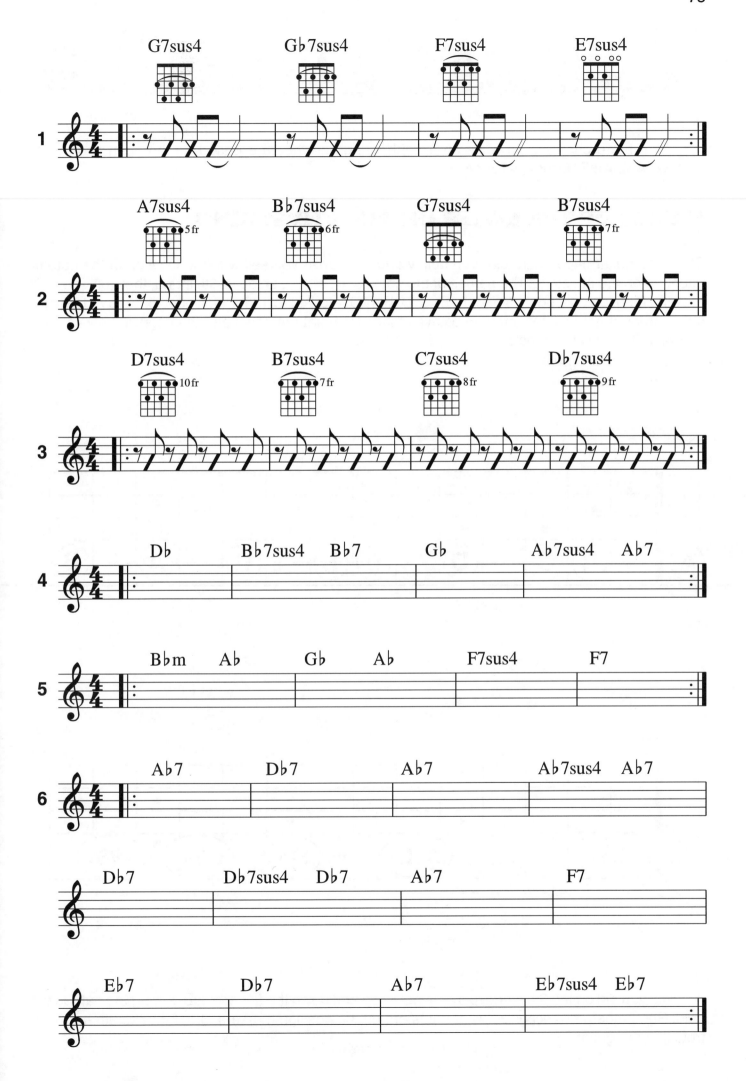

A-FORM BARRE CHORDS

A-form barre chords have roots on the 5th string and they are based on the open chords: **A, A7, Am, Am7, Asus4, A7sus4**.

NAMES OF THE NOTES ON THE 5TH STRING

Study the guitar fingerboard diagram below and familiarize yourself with the location of the note in each fret on the 5th string. The names of the notes start with A, an open 5th string, then just like with the 6th string, go up alphabetically: A, B, C, D, E, F, G, etc. At the 12th fret, it goes back to A, then the same order of notes is repeated an octave higher. Both natural notes and the notes in between the natural notes are shown below:

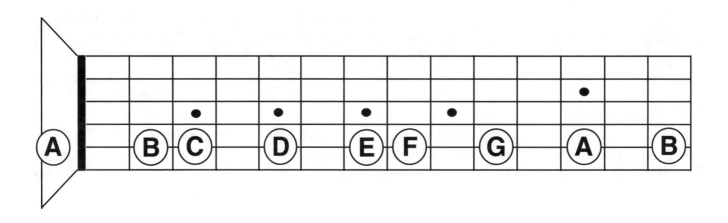

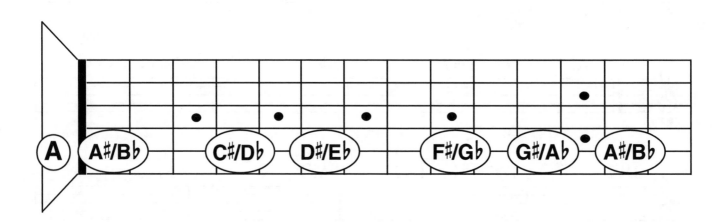

Just like you did on the 6th string, play the notes up and down the fingerboard, saying the names out loud. Remember and recognize what notes are on the position markers, 3rd, 5th, 7th, 9th and 12th frets on your guitar.

3-7

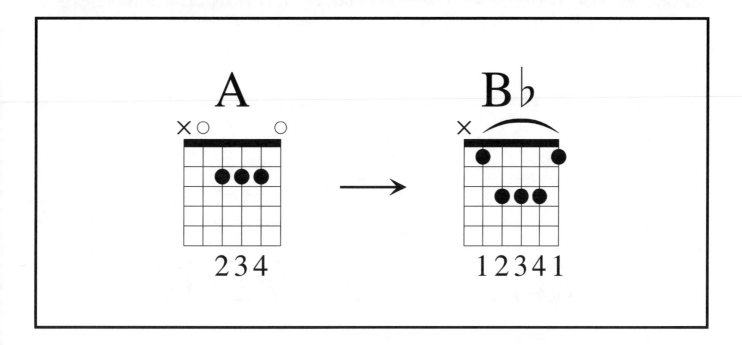

Play the A chord without changing the fingerings. Keep your hand in the same shape and slide it up one fret so that your 1st finger forms a barre across the 1st fret to play a B♭ chord as shown.

Alternatively, an A-form chord is sometimes played with either a 3rd- or 4th-finger barre. The three notes on the 4th, 3rd and 2nd strings are held down by flattening the 3rd or 4th finger into a smaller half-barre as shown below.

ALTERNATIVE FINGERINGS

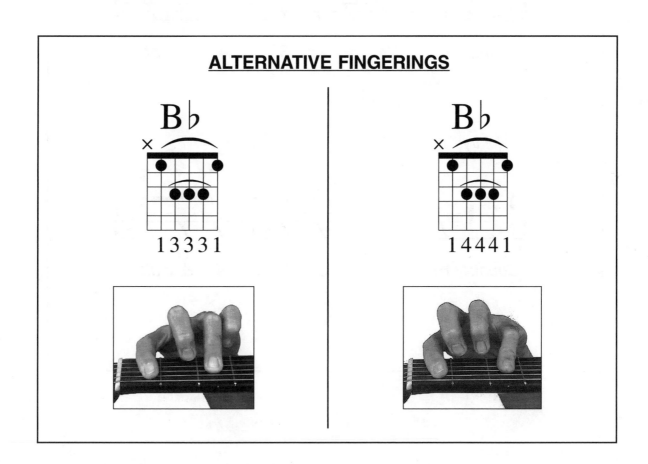

The strumming patterns introduce an *eighth-note triplet* slash which represents three notes played in the space of one beat or count. Tap your foot in the same manner as before on the first, second, third and fourth beats, and count **ONE-&-ah, TWO-&-ah, THREE-&-ah, FOUR-&-ah** (You can also say ONE-two-three, TWO-two-three, THREE-two-three, FOUR-two-three). Use all downstrokes or alternate downstrokes and upstrokes as shown or experiment on your own.

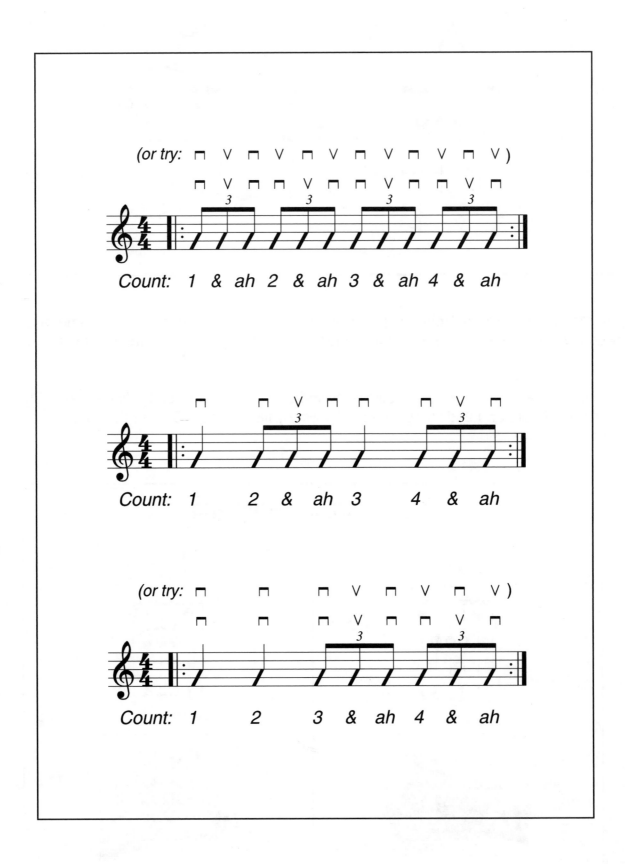

3-8

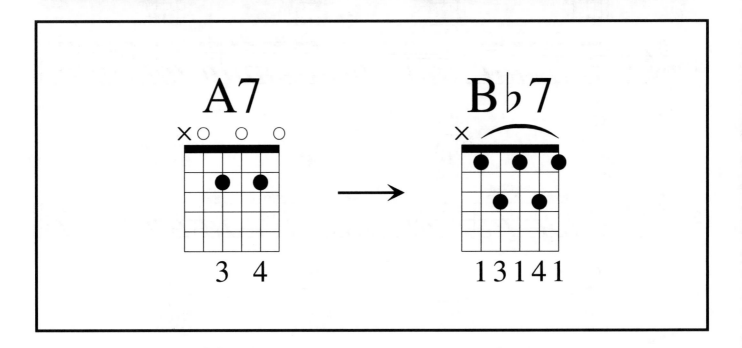

P lay the A7 chord using your 4th finger on the 2nd fret of the 2nd string and 3rd finger on the 2nd fret of the 4th string. Shift the shape, barring with your 1st finger along the fingerboard. Since your 2nd finger is free, you can support the barre by placing it above the 1st finger. The strumming patterns are well used in rock and blues; they are called a *shuffled* rhythm. First, practice alternating downstrokes and upstrokes as shown. Then, try each pattern with consecutive downstrokes as typically done in this style.

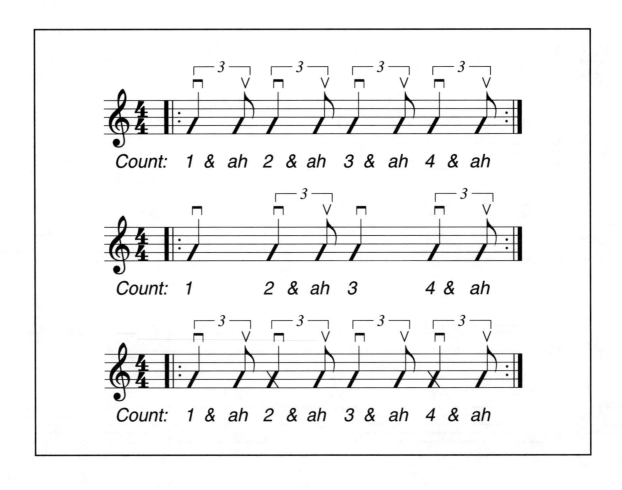

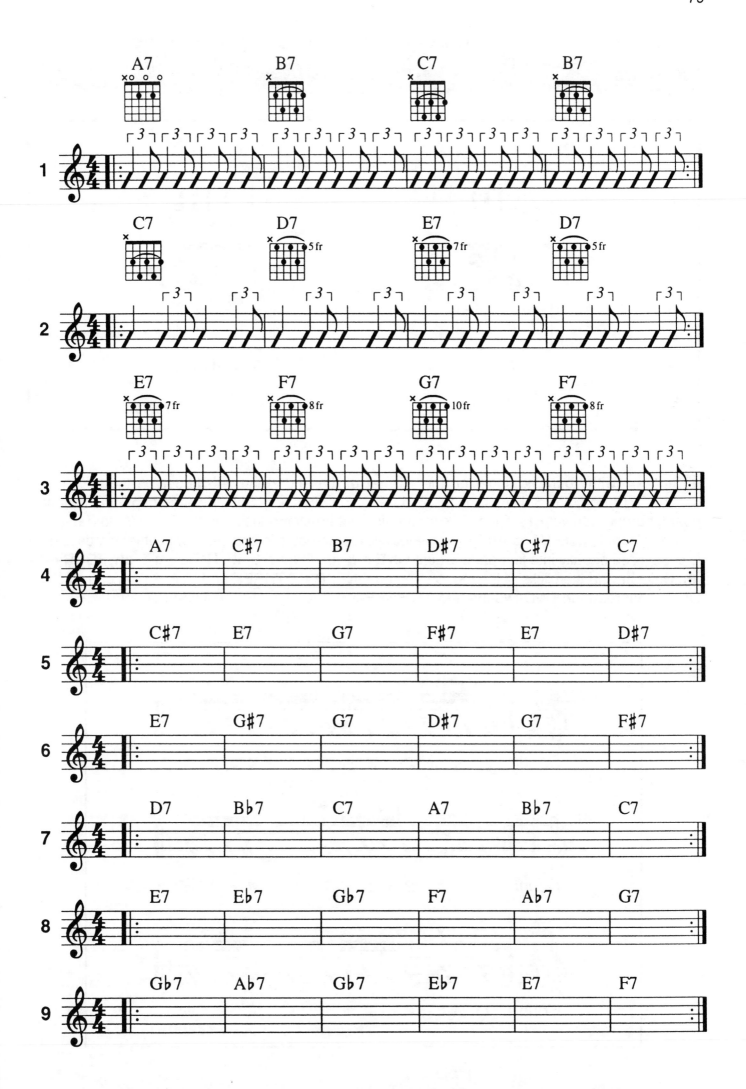

3-9

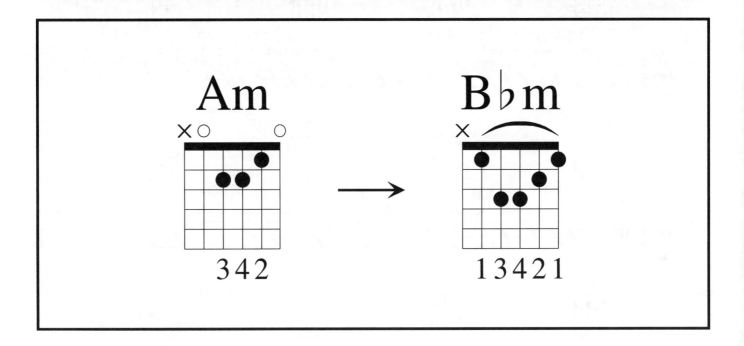

Play Am with your 2nd finger on the 1st fret of the 2nd string, 4th finger on the 2nd fret of the 3rd string, and 3rd finger on the 2nd fret of the 4th string. Shift the Am-shape up the fingerboard, barring with your 1st finger. The strumming patterns introduce you to *sixteenth-note* slashes. A sixteenth-note gets **1/4 count**. There are four sixteenth-notes in one beat, or in other words, a beat is subdivided equally into four parts. Count **ONE-e-&-ah, TWO-e-&-ah, THREE-e-&-ah, FOUR-e-&-ah,** while having the clicks of the metronome on ONE, TWO, THREE and FOUR (You can also say ONE-two-three-four, TWO-two-three-four, THREE-two-three-four, FOUR-two-three-four).

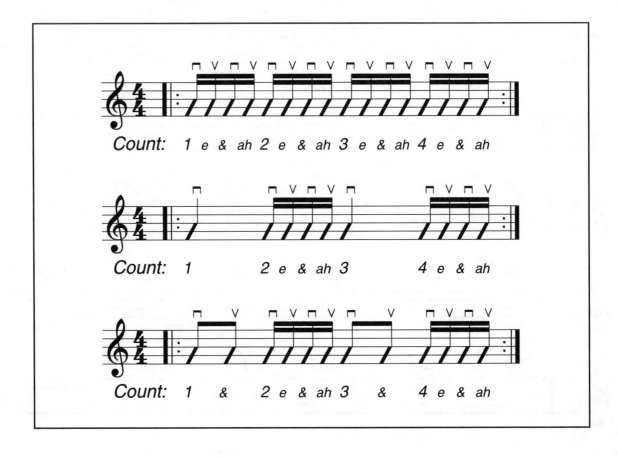

Take a chord and play each pattern repeatedly following the strumming directions as shown. Strive to divide a beat by four *equal* parts. A symbol, ⅟ in the exercises means to repeat the previous measure.

3-10

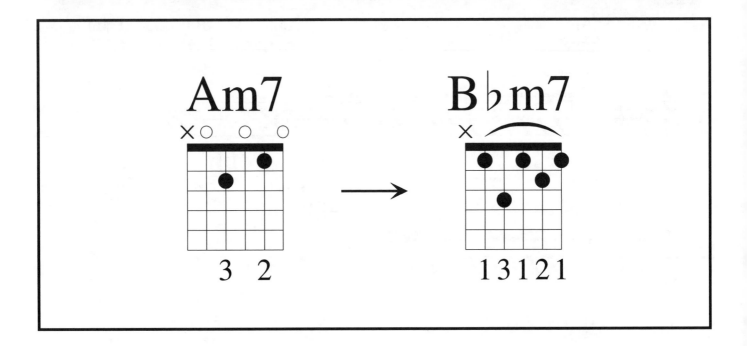

Play Am7 with your 2nd finger on the 1st fret of the 2nd string and 3rd finger on the 2nd fret of the 4th string. Shift the shape, barring with your 1st finger. The strumming patterns combine eighth-note and sixteenth-note slashes. If you have trouble getting the feel of the sixteenth-note, set your metronome so that each click would be equal to a sixteenth note. At the same time, keep tapping your foot on every four clicks, still counting and hearing each click as ONE-e-&-ah, TWO-e-&-ah, THREE-e-&-ah, FOUR-e-&-ah.

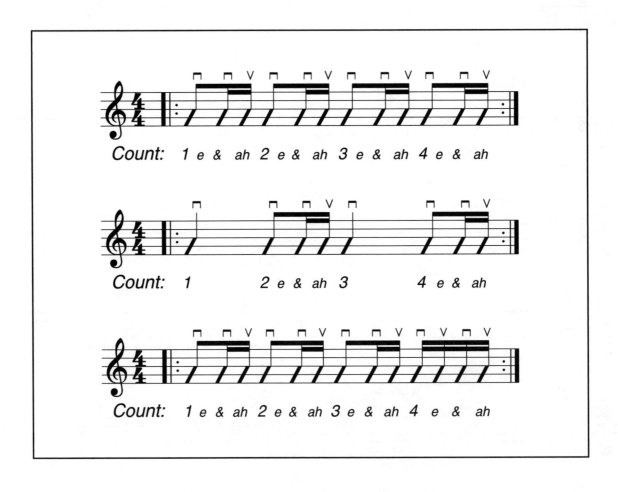

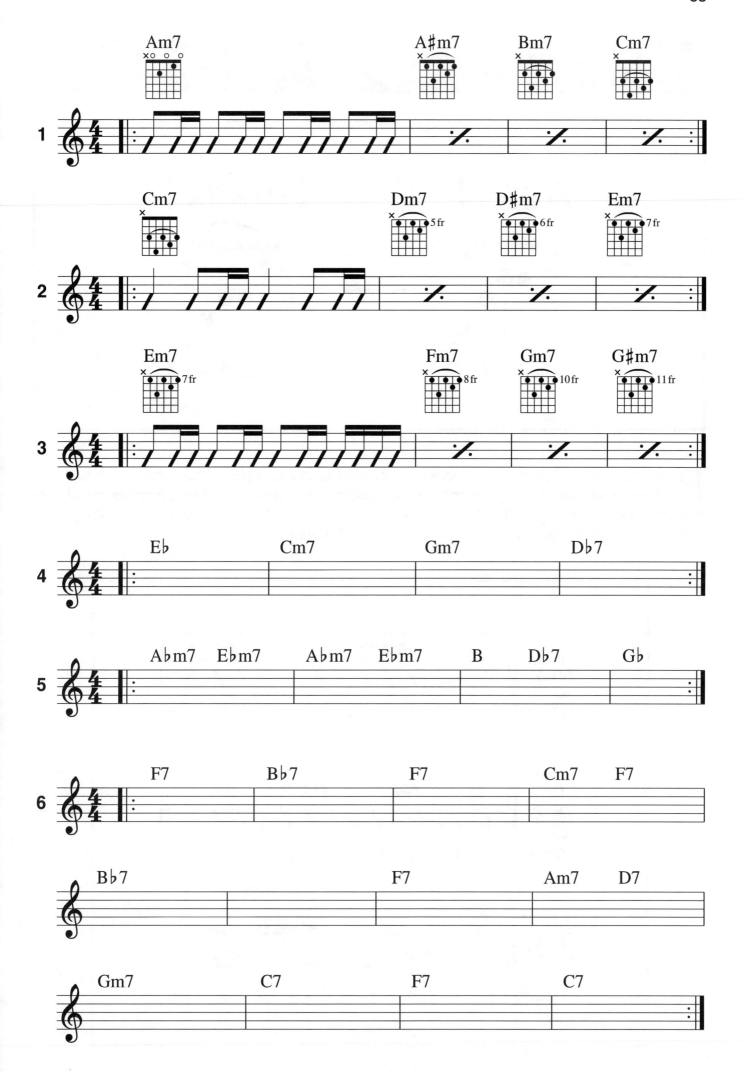

3-11

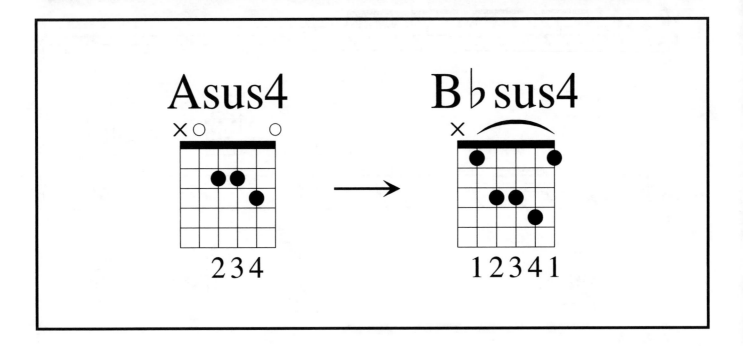

Asus4   →   B♭sus4

Play Asus4 without changing the fingerings. Simply keep your hand in the same shape and shift it, barring with your 1st finger, along the fingerboard. The strumming patterns combine the eighth-note and sixteenth-note slightly different from the previous section. Take your time to study each pattern well. Play it slowly and repeatedly until you get it right.

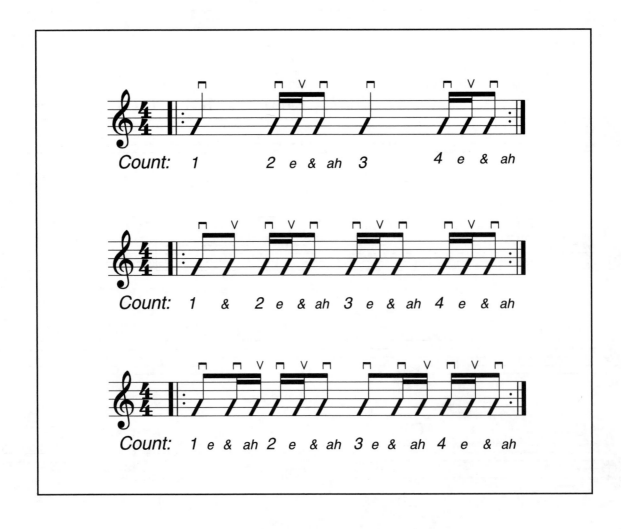

Count: 1   2 e & ah 3   4 e & ah

Count: 1 & 2 e & ah 3 e & ah 4 e & ah

Count: 1 e & ah 2 e & ah 3 e & ah 4 e & ah

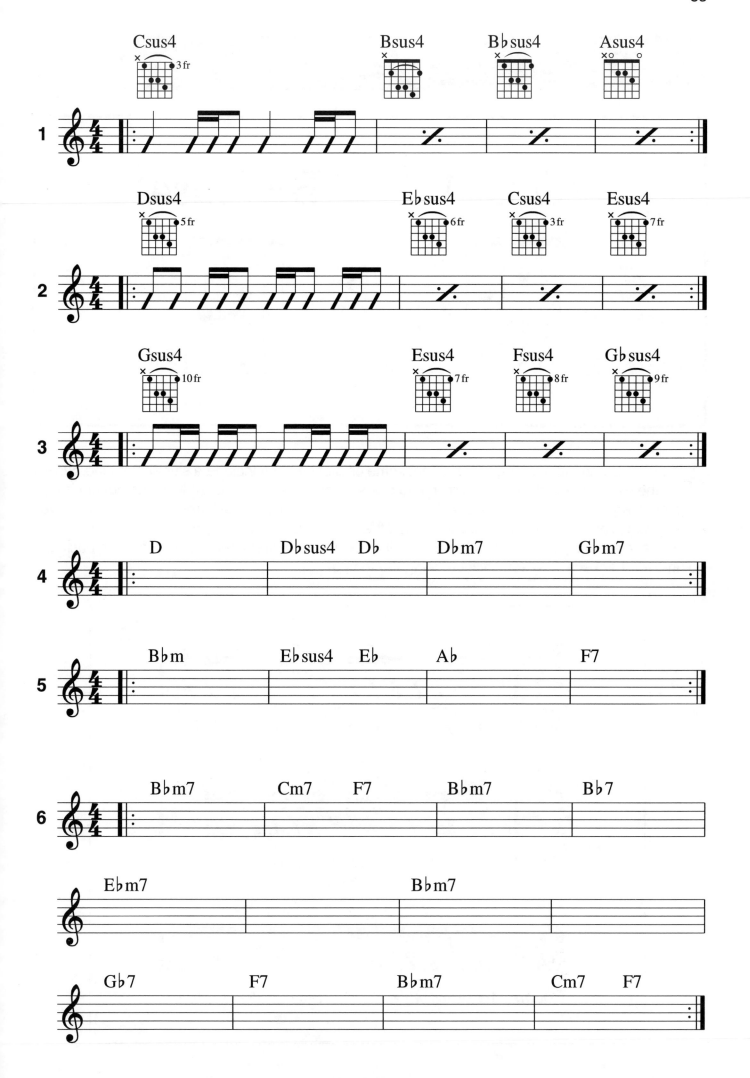

3-12

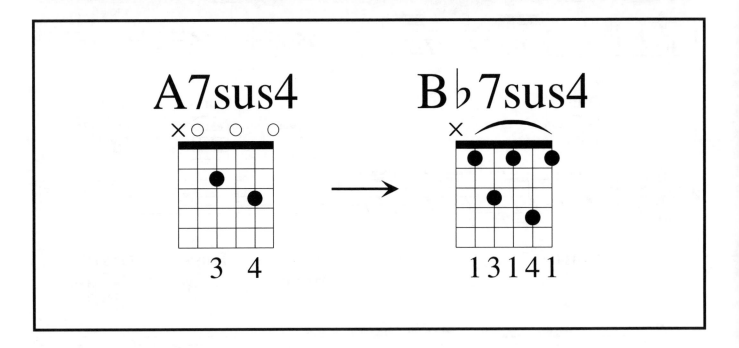

The last strumming patterns may present some challenge; they include a slur and muting. Slow it all the way down and take enough time to digest each pattern well. Even if you do not get it right the first time, do not worry about it. Take a day or a few days off, come back fresh and try it again even more *slowly*. This suggestion applies to all the other exercises; whenever you have a new challenge, do not get discouraged even if you cannot get it correctly at the first attempt. Keep coming back and going over them slowly, gradually increasing the tempo.

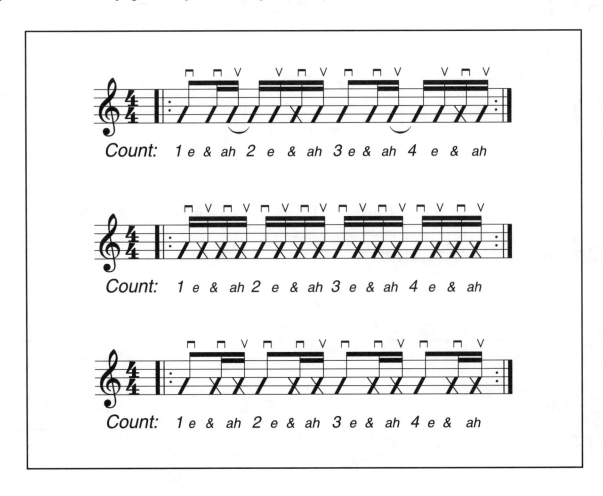

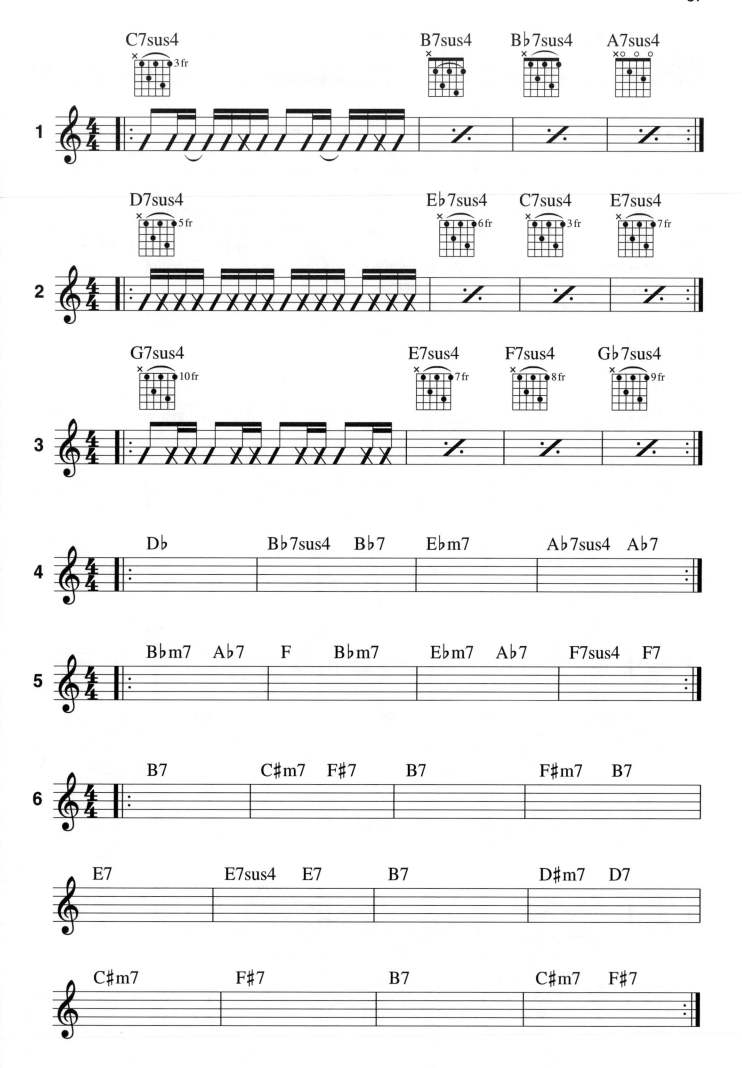

CHAPTER 3 REVIEW

To reinforce your learning, go back and review all the chords and the strumming patterns presented in this chapter. Choose a pattern and play it through each exercise. Or write out several patterns of your choice, combining them in any way you like. Always remember to use a metronome, count and tap, and sustain each slash fully for appropriate counts. Isolate and practice slowly and repeatedly those places where you have difficulties moving from one chord to another. Notice that there is more than one way to play each exercise by combining open chords and several different barre chords. Practice as many combinations as possible. At the end, you'll find a song, *Old Folks At Home* arranged in rock style with an accompaniment example. Experiment with different patterns and create your own accompaniment.

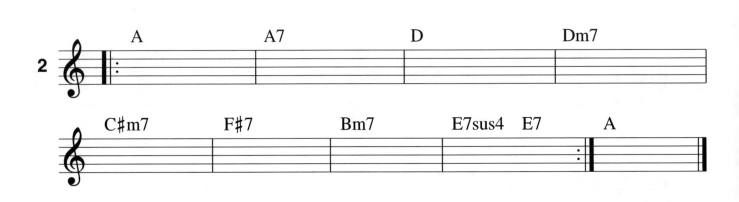

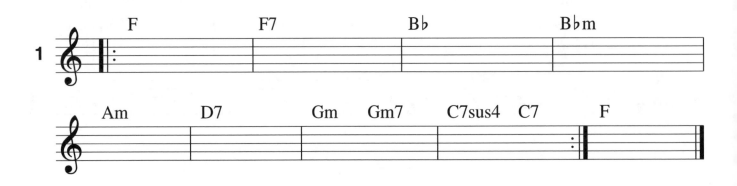

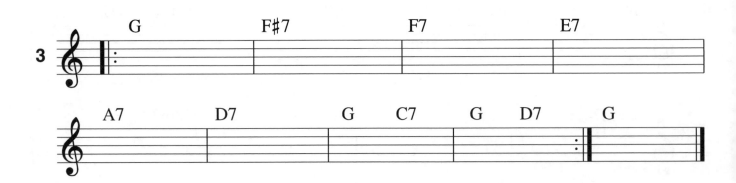

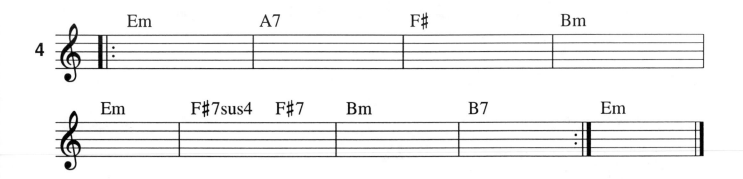

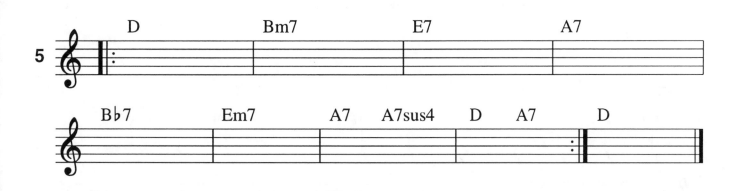

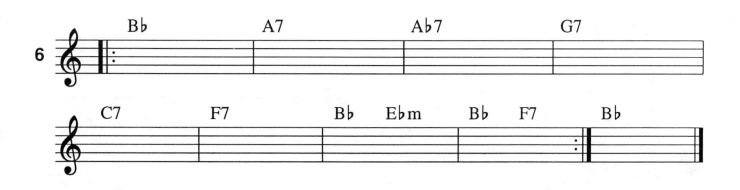

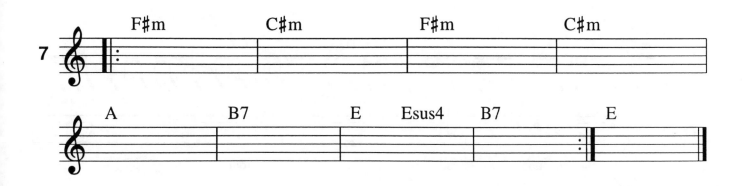

OLD FOLKS AT HOME

Rock ♩ = 76

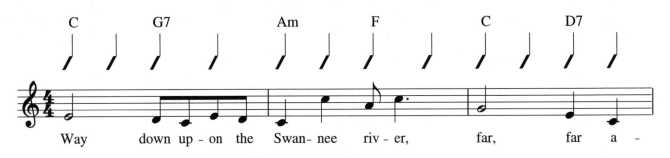

Way down up-on the Swan-nee riv - er, far, far a -

way; there's where my heart is turn - ing ev -er,

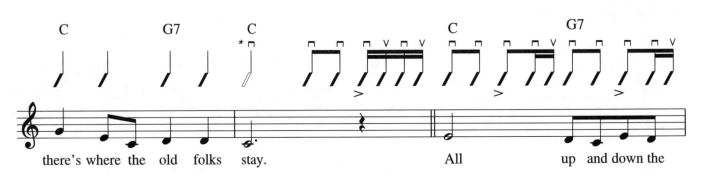

there's where the old folks stay. All up and down the

Suggested strumming directions.

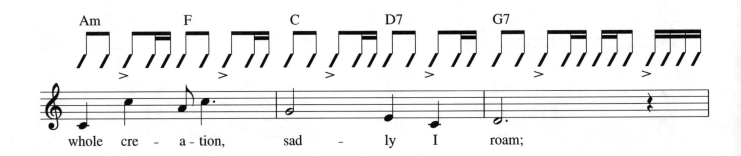

whole cre - a -tion, sad - ly I roam;

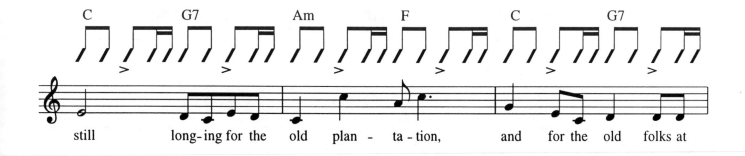

still long-ing for the old plan - ta - tion, and for the old folks at

home. All the world is sad and drear - y

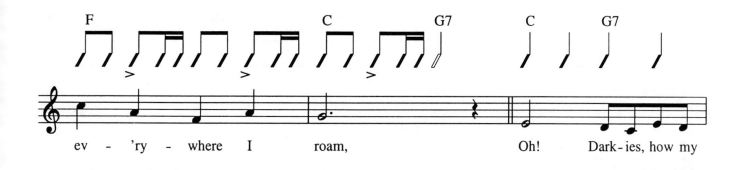

ev - 'ry - where I roam, Oh! Dark-ies, how my

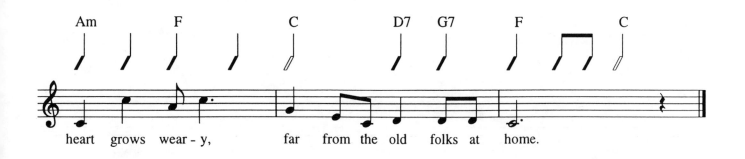

heart grows wear-y, far from the old folks at home.

Write out and practice your own chord progressions.

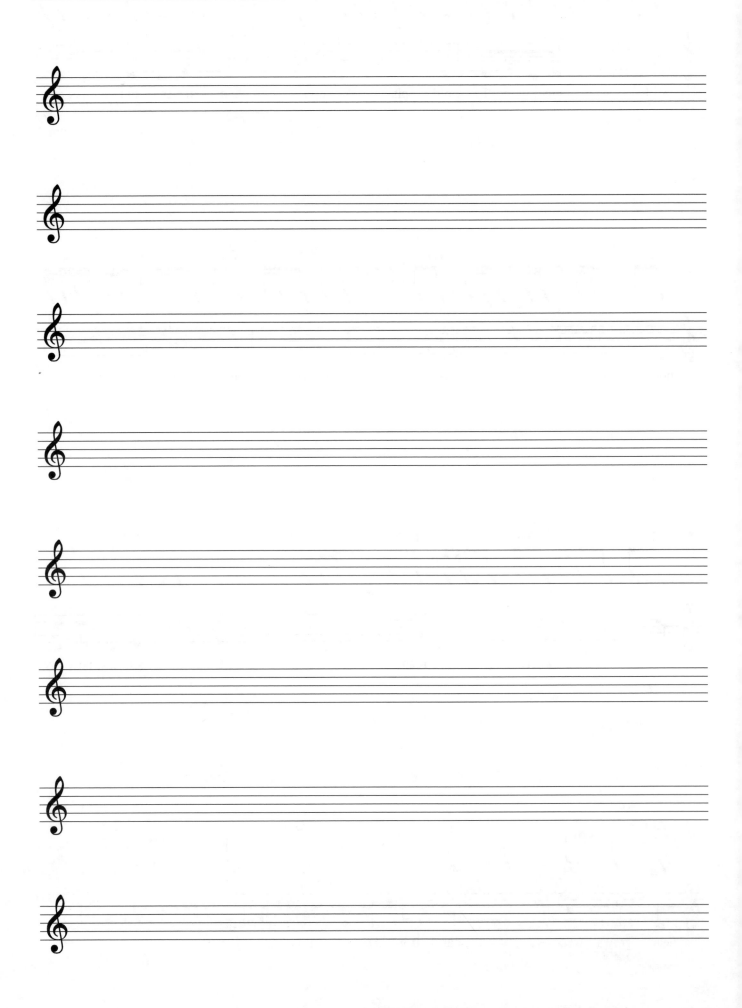

CHAPTER 4
OTHER OPEN CHORDS AND FINGERSTYLE

In the next two chapters, you are going to learn a new accompaniment technique called *fingerstyle*. It was given this name because the style involves the use of your right-hand fingers instead of a pick. The style has been used for hundreds of years in classical music. It was widely adapted and has been incorporated into folk, rock, country and many other types of music. As far as the chords are concerned, you will learn other well used open chords: *major 7th, major 6th, sus2, augmented 7th, diminished 7th, minor 7b5, minor (major7), minor 6th.* Below are again some things to go over before the exercises.

RIGHT HAND

Right-hand Letters

The letters to indicate each finger of the right-hand are shown below:

p : Thumb
i : 1st finger
m : 2nd finger
a : 3rd finger

Basic Position

As with strumming, experiment with several positions and find the one most comfortable for you. As a reference, the classical hand position, the basis of all the others, is shown below. With the thumb (*p*) resting either on the 6th or 5th string, place the tips of your 1st (*i*), 2nd (*m*) and 3rd (*a*) fingers on the three highest strings: *i* on the 3rd string, *m* on the 2nd and *a* on the 1st string. Your wrist and the strings will be at or near a 90-degree angle.

Normally, the thumb (*p*) is used to hit the bass strings (6th, 5th and 4th) with a downstroke. Using upstrokes, the 1st finger (*i*) plays the 3rd string, the 2nd (*m*) finger plays the 2nd string, and the 3rd (*a*) finger plays the 1st string.

THUMBPICKS AND FINGERPICKS

Classical and many fingerstyle guitarists traditionally keep the nails on their right hand long and use them to pick the strings. Some people, on the other hand, choose to use metal or plastic thumbpicks and fingerpicks shown below.

RIGHT HAND WITH THUMBPICK AND FINGERPICKS

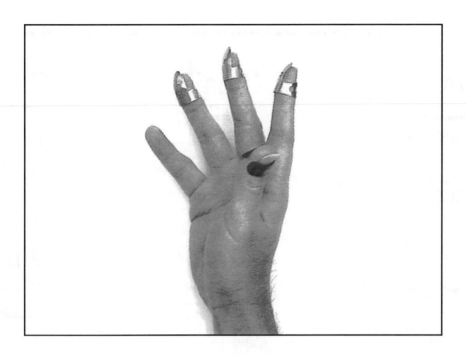

TAB

A *tablature* or TAB is a six-line staff graphically showing the fingerboard. Each of the six lines represents one of the guitar strings as shown below. The numbers that appear on the lines are *fret* numbers indicating where to press down. "0" means open string, "1" means the 1st fret, "2" means the 2nd fret and so on. Notice that TAB does not tell you the rhythms of how each note is to be played so that you still have to be able to recognize and read the rhythms from the conventional staff. However TAB has become increasingly popular and widely used and it is a helpful aid when used in conjunction with the regular notation. TAB will be placed just below the regular staff.

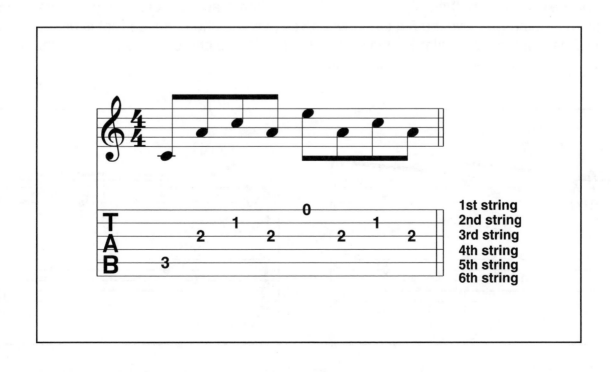

4·1

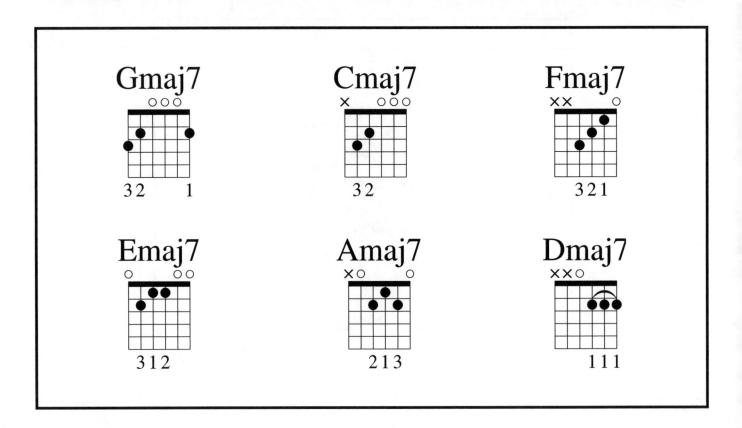

In this section, you are going to learn six *major 7th* chords and four basic fingerstyle patterns. First look at each chord diagram, follow the fingering carefully, and play each chord. Major 7th is often abbreviated and written as **maj7** or **△7** or **MA7**. This book will use maj7.

As for the accompaniment patterns, this chapter will show various fingerstyle patterns, called *arpeggios*. Arpeggios are played by holding a chord and then hitting one note after another in sequence. The four patterns are shown here. Follow the right-hand fingering carefully and play each pattern very slowly until you master it flawlessly with a metronome. Play all patterns using the Cmaj7 chord as shown below, then try them with other major 7th chords as well. One thing to note is that, in general, the thumb (p) plays the 6th string when you play the chord whose root is on the 6th string such as Emaj7 or Gmaj7. Similarly, *p* plays the 5th string for the chord whose root is on the 5th string and it plays the 4th string when the root of the chord is on the 4th string.

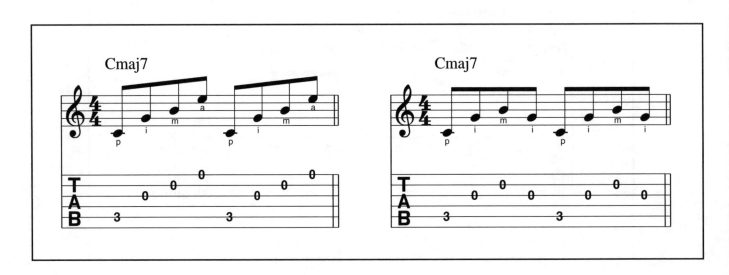

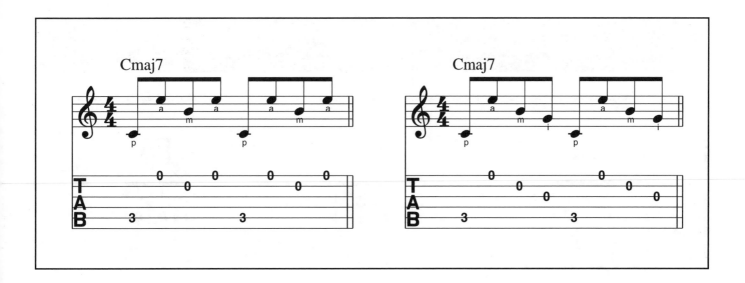

When you become comfortable with playing the above arpeggios, try the following exercises. As shown in #1, you can play it through the progression using only one pattern or you can combine several patterns of your choice.

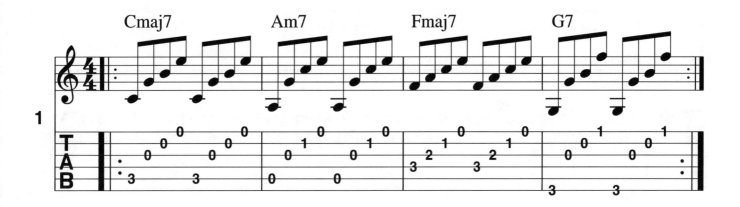

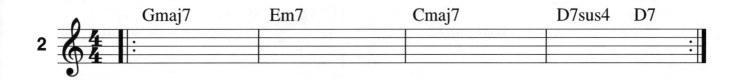

4-2

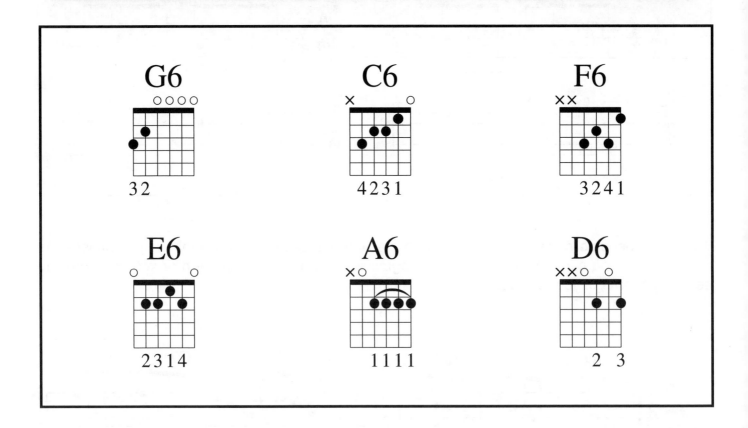

This section introduces six *major 6th* chords and four arpeggios. Major 6th is written as **MA 6** or simply **6**. Study each chord diagram and arpeggio pattern well and follow the fingerings carefully.

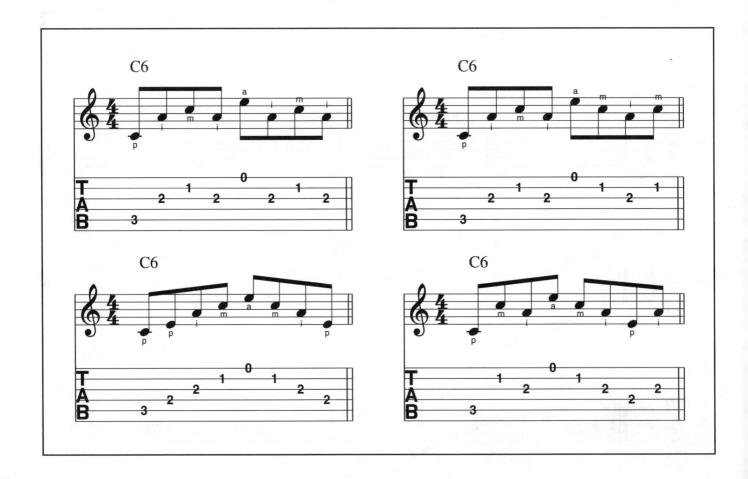

After you become comfortable with playing the above arpeggios, try the following exercises. Either play an exercise through using one pattern as shown in #1 or combine several patterns of your choice in any order.

1

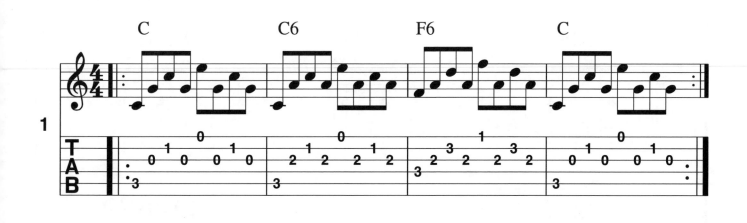

2

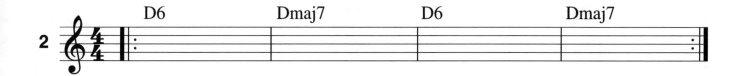

3

4

5

6

4-3

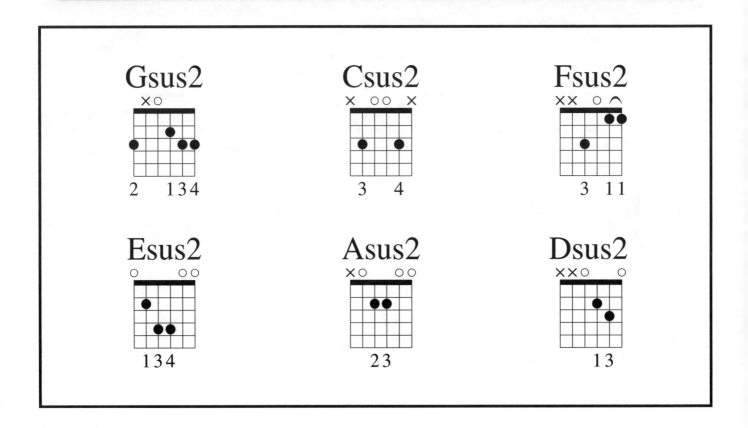

In this section, six *sus2* chords and four arpeggios are presented. Notice that when playing the following arpeggios, you are to start by using two fingers, either *p* and *a* or *p* and *m*, *simultaneously*. Practice very slowly until the two notes are struck and played with a perfect sync. In addition, on the 3rd and 4th patterns, the roots of the chords are on slightly different places than usual, creating somewhat different feelings.

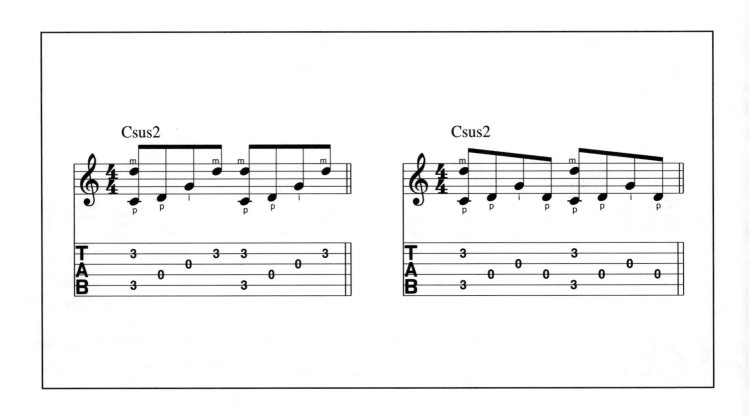

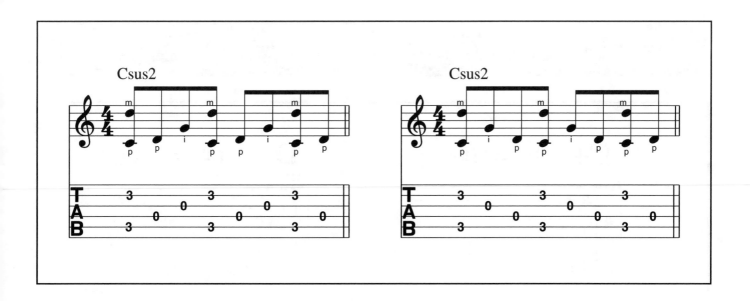

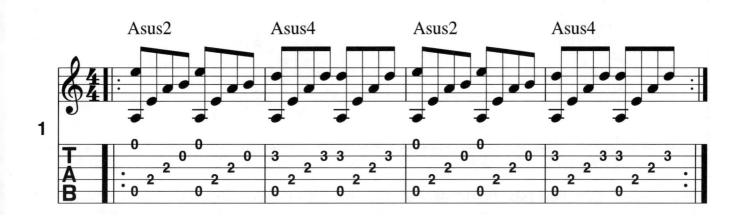

4·4

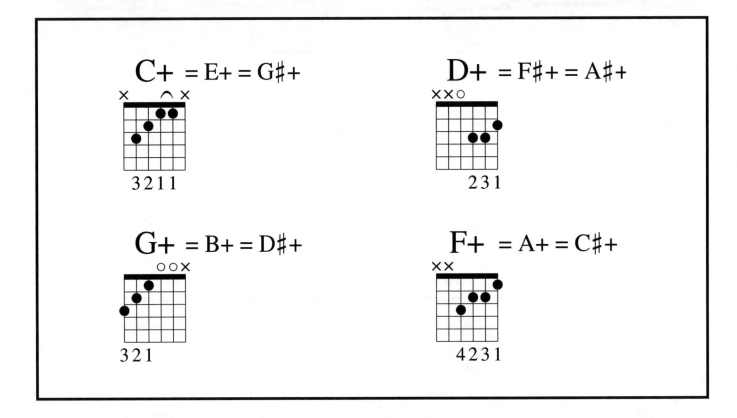

$C+ = E+ = G\sharp+$

x   x

3 2 1 1

$D+ = F\sharp+ = A\sharp+$

x x o

2 3 1

$G+ = B+ = D\sharp+$

o o x

3 2 1

$F+ = A+ = C\sharp+$

x x

4 2 3 1

You may find the next two chord types, *augmented 7th* and *diminished 7th* chords, unique and special. Because of the structure of the chord, any note in the chord can be a root of the chord. For example, C augmented or C+ (**+** or **aug.** are usually used as an abbreviation for augmented) consists of C, E and G♯. Look at the chord diagram and play C+ at the 1st position. Now play exactly the same shape at the 5th fret with your 3rd finger on the E note. You will see that even if your root is not C, each note of this chord is exactly the same as when you had the C+ at the 1st position: C, E and G♯. The same is true when you play G♯+ at the 9th fret; the chord consists of the same notes: C, E and G♯. This means that C+, E+ and G♯+ are exactly the same chord with a different starting point!

For details, refer to a theory book which explains this unique property of an augmented chord, but for now just remember that there exists only four augmented chords: C+, G+, F+ and D+. And each chord is exactly the same as *two* other chords as shown above. As explained in the *Enharmonic Notation* section (*see p. 19*), it is possible to write G♯+ as A♭+ or F♯+ as G♭+. Similarly, A♯+ is the same chord as B♭+, D♯+ equals to E♭+, and C♯+ and D♭+ are exactly the same chords.

As for the selected arpeggios, notice that all include a two-note part which is played by *m* and *a* simultaneously. The 3rd pattern starts with a three-note part played by three fingers, *p*, *m* and *a*. Isolate and practice these parts very slowly until you can play the two or three notes at exactly the same time without hearing them separately.

When you are comfortable playing each arpeggio, move on to the exercises. As before, either play each exercise through using one pattern as shown or combine several patterns in any way you like.

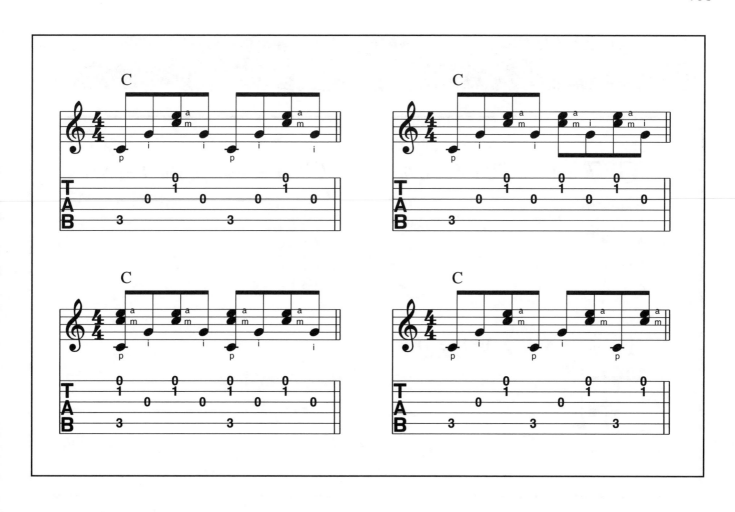

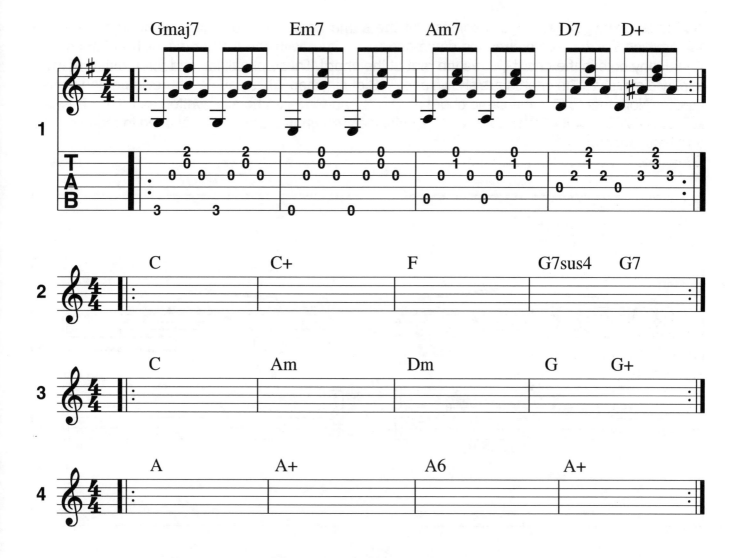

4-5

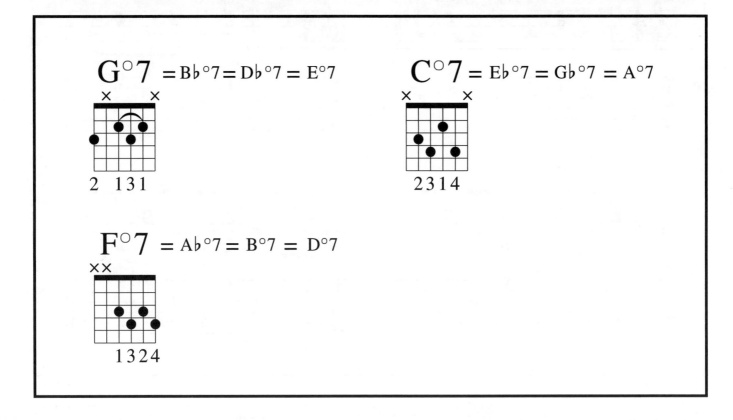

Just as an augmented chord consists of the same notes as two other augmented chords, a *diminished 7th* chord shares the same chord structure with *three* other diminished 7th chords. Again, any note in the chord can be the root of the chord. These pluralities and three different ways to play diminished 7th chords are shown above. C diminished 7th is usually abbreviated and written as **C°7**. Note that E♭°7 is the same chord as D#°7. And G♭°7 can be also written as F#°7. Likewise, A♭°7 = G#°7, B♭°7= A#°7 and D♭°7=C#°7. Diminished 7th chords are popularly used in many of jazz and Latin songs.

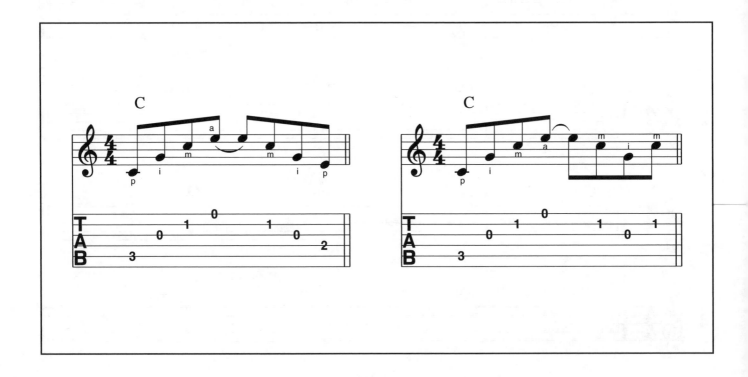

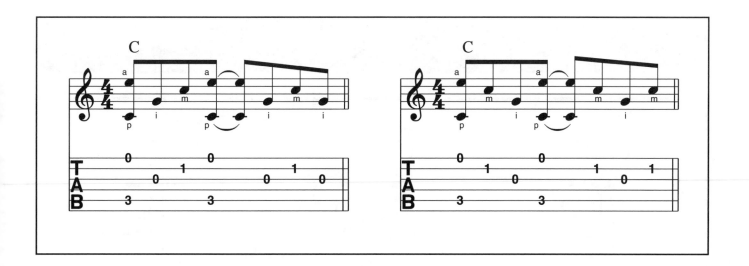

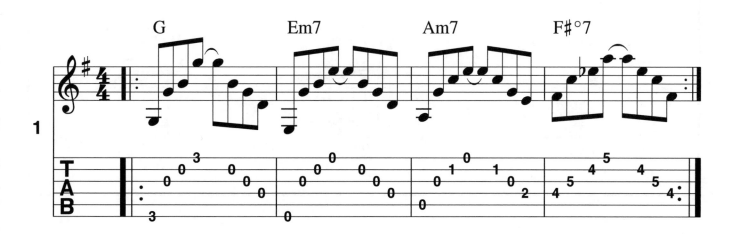

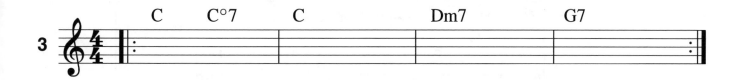

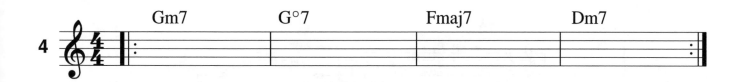

4-6

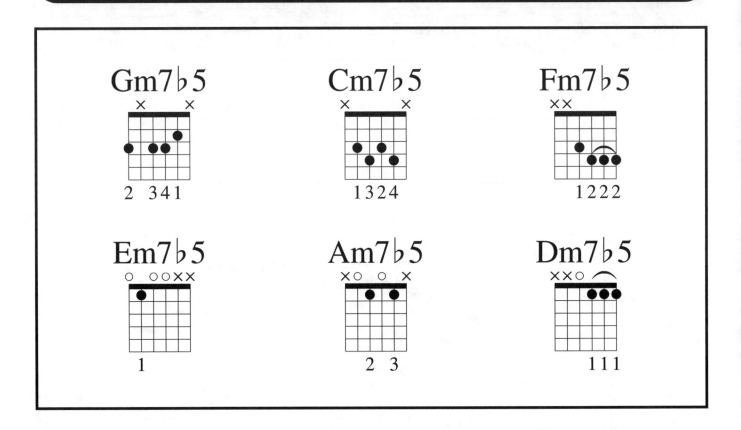

Gm7♭5   Cm7♭5   Fm7♭5

Em7♭5   Am7♭5   Dm7♭5

Minor 7♭5 is normally notated as **m7♭5** and occasionally as **Ø7**. Notice all the arpeggios introduced here consist of eighth-note triplets. Make sure you divide each beat or click of a metronome equally by three. Practice each pattern very slowly until you can execute each triplet flawlessly.

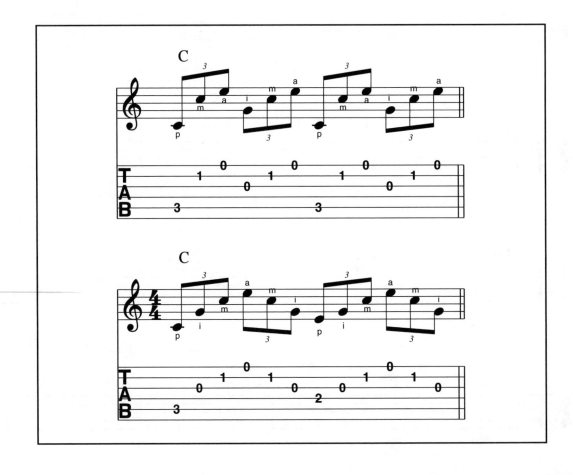

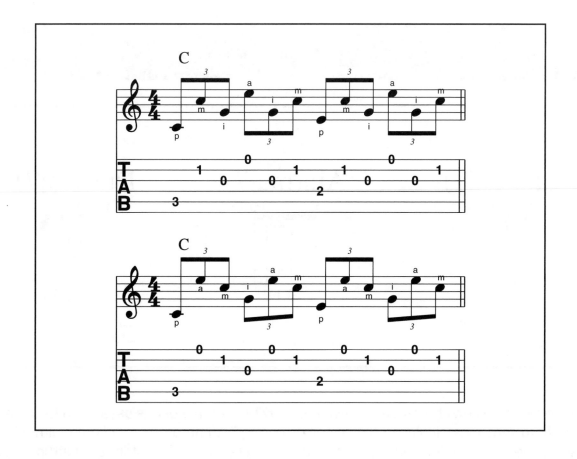

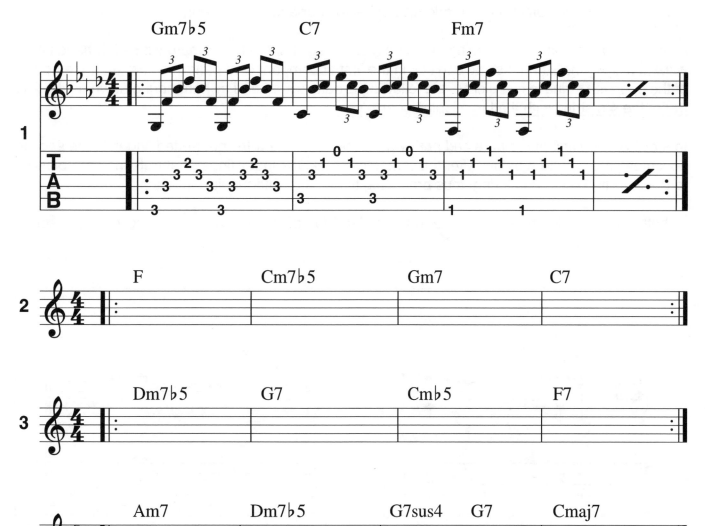

4-7

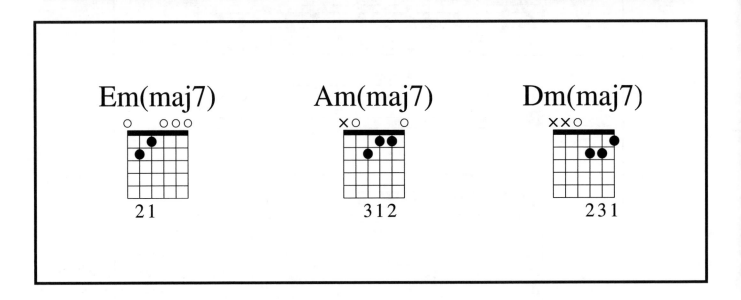

Em(maj7)   Am(maj7)   Dm(maj7)

Here are the three new chords, called *minor (major7)*. Minor (major7) is usually written as **m(maj7)**. The chord functions similar to the minor or minor 7th chords. The accompaniment patterns below show the two new techniques unique to the guitar and other stringed instruments, called *hammer-on* and *pull-off* which can add nice spice to your accompaniment.

A *hammer-on* consists of slamming or hitting a string against the fingerboard with a left-hand finger without picking the string. As you can see in the first accompaniment pattern below, after the note D of the open 4th string is first picked, the following E note is sounded by hammering down on the 2nd fret of the 4th string with the left middle finger.

In a *pull-off,* you first pick a note and *pull away* to the next note with your fretted finger. In the second accompaniment pattern below, after the C note is struck, the index finger that frets the note *pulls off* to the unfretted open 2nd string, thus producing the B note without picking again.

In both cases, make sure to hammer-on or pull-off forcefully so that the second note will sound clearly.

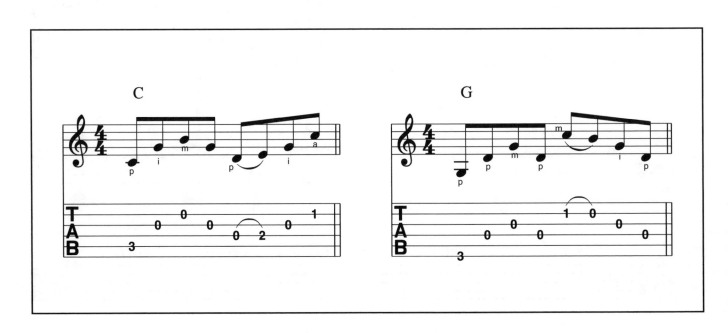

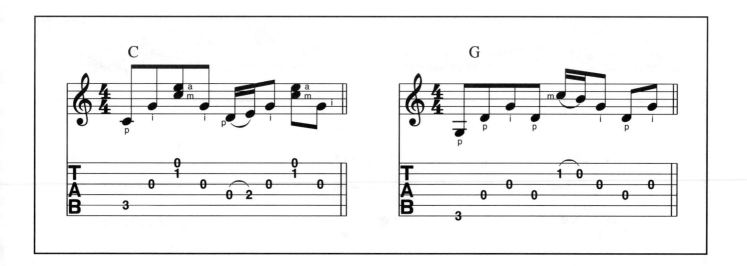

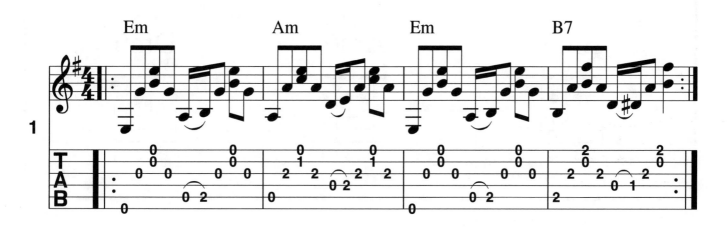

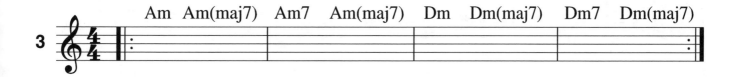

4-8

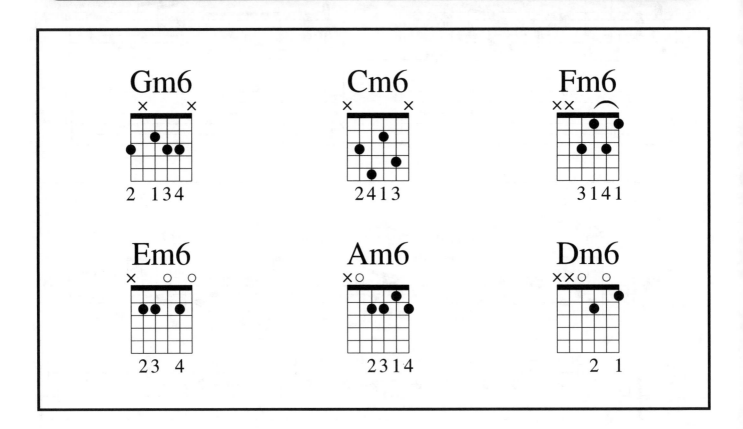

In this section, six *minor 6th* chords and four arpeggios in 3/4 meter are presented. Minor 6th is normally written as **m6**. Again study each chord diagram and follow the fingering carefully. You have already played all the arpeggios presented here. Each is slightly modified so that it can be played in 3/4 meter.

After you become comfortable with playing these arpeggios, try the following exercises. Either play an exercise through using one pattern as shown in #1 or combine several patterns of your choice in any order.

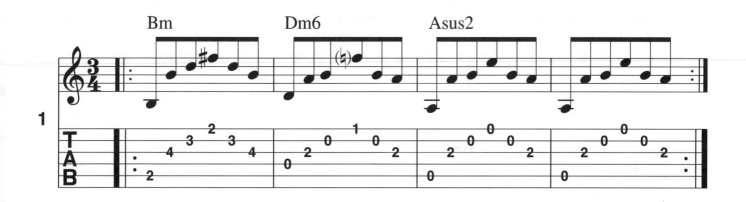

CHAPTER 4 REVIEW

This review section includes some chord progressions utilizing some of the chords you have learned throughout this chapter. Review all chords and patterns first. Write out any accompaniment styles or play it from your memory. At the end, you'll find a song, *Silent Night* with an accompaniment example. Feel free to experiment with different patterns and chords and create your own accompaniment.

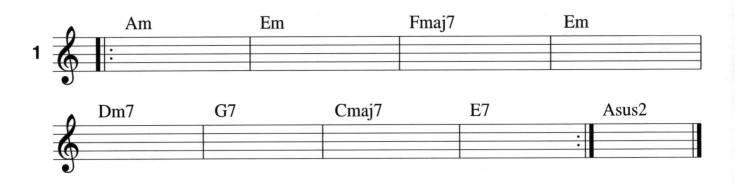

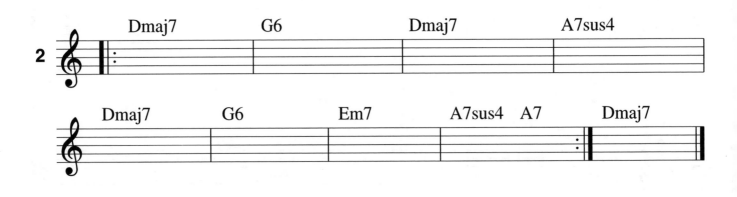

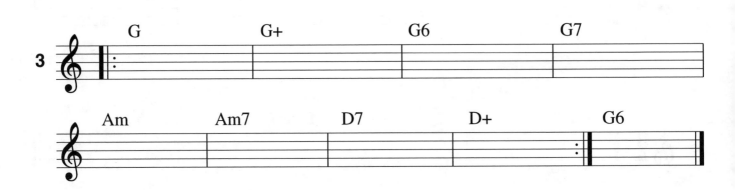

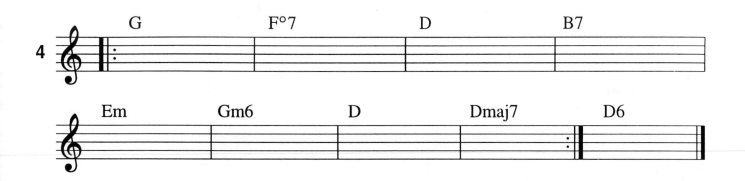

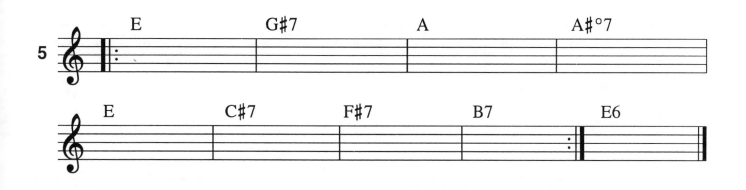

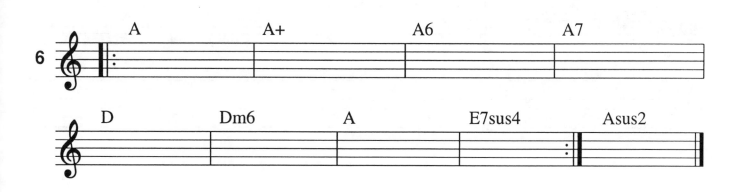

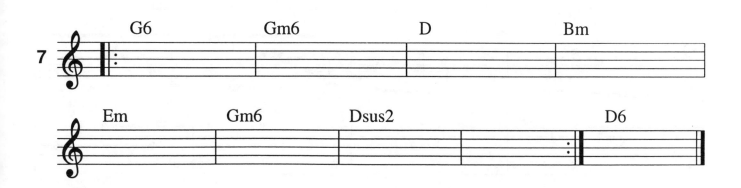

SILENT NIGHT

Slowly

1. Si - lent night! Ho - ly night!

All is calm, all is bright.

Round you Vir - gin Moth - er and Child.

Additional Lyrics

2. Silent night! Holy Night!
   Shepherds quake at the sight!
   Glories stream from heaven afar;
   Heavenly hosts sing, "Alleluia!
   Christ, the Savior, is born!
   Christ, the Savior is born!"

3. Silent night! Holy night!
   Song of God, love's pure light!
   Radiant beams from Thy holy face
   With the dawn of redeeming grace,
   Jesus, Lord, at They birth!
   Jesus, Lord, at Thy birth!

Write out and practice your own chord progressions.

CHAPTER 5

SLASH CHORDS, CARTER FAMILY AND FINGER-PICKING

Sometimes you see a chord name with a slash over a different bass note than the root, such as C/G, G/B, Em/D, D7/A, etc. The symbol left of the slash represents the chord, and the one right of the slash indicates the bass note. C/G (*C over G*), for instance, means you play a C chord with G in the bass. G/B (*G over B*) is a G chord with B in the bass. A chord over a different bass note, or a *slash chord* as it is usually called, is often used to create a certain bass movement: a forward movement, ascending, descending or static. It can be also inserted in a chord progression to create a smooth transition from one chord to another. And sometimes it is used for its own unique sound. The use of this type of chord has been very popular in almost any kind of music, including pop, rock, country or jazz.

As for the accompaniment styles, you are going to learn the *Carter Family Style,* or simply *Carter Style*—a strumming pattern widely used in country, bluegrass and folk music. Also, an additional fingerstyle known as *finger-picking* or *Travis-picking* is presented.

SOME COMMON SLASH CHORDS

On the next two pages are charts that summarize some typical and common slash chords. As you will notice, you are already familiar with all the chords written left of the slash; all you need to do is to play a chord you know over a bass note different from the one you would normally play. This means that you can create a slash chord on the spot even if you have never seen it before! The charts presented here list only a common way to play each slash chord. Many other approaches to voice the same slash chord exist. After you have gone through each one of them and once you understand how it is built, experiment and find something different and original.

SOME COMMON MAJOR SLASH CHORDS

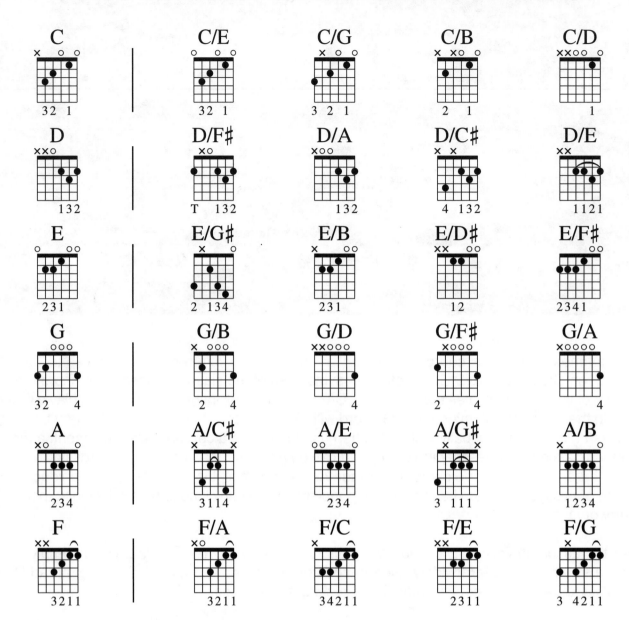

SOME COMMON MINOR SLASH CHORDS

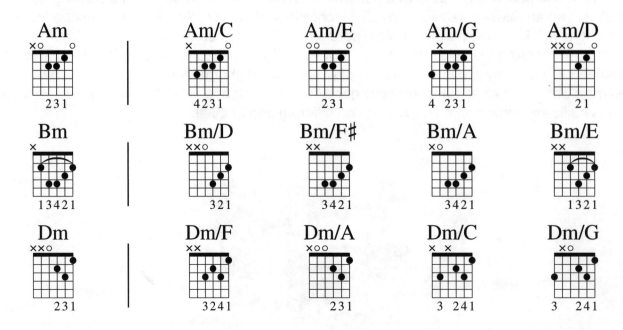

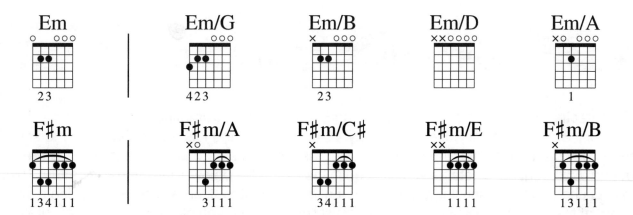

SOME COMMON DOMINANT 7TH SLASH CHORDS

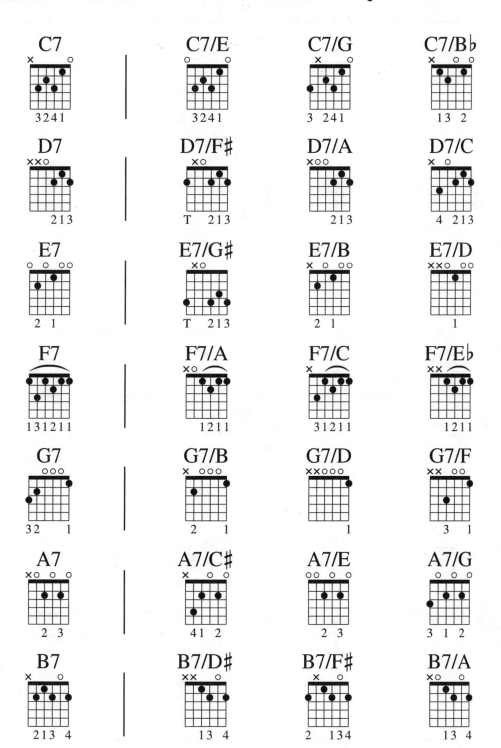

5·1

This section introduces a very popular and widely used strumming pattern called the *Carter Family Style*. It is mostly used in country, bluegrass, rag and folk music. Basically the style consists of playing a bass note and strumming chords. The bass note is often alternated between the root and a different bass note as you can see in the examples below. Play the basic patterns using C and C/G chords first as shown. You may find it a little difficult to alternate between a single note and a chord at first. If that is the case, start *very slowly* making sure you play each pattern accurately and steadily. The Carter Family Style is usually played with a pick, but you can also play with fingers: the thumb picks out the bass notes while the 1st or both 1st and 2nd fingers together strum the chords.

Try the following progressions using one or combinations of any of the Carter Family Style patterns. The two examples show how the Carter Family Style can be played with extensive bass runs. The three notes written before the first repeat sign are called *pick-up* notes. Count off ONE-TWO-THREE-FOUR and begin playing on beat TWO.

5-2

The accompaniment style in the next two sections is called *finger-picking* or *Travis-picking* (named after the country legend, Merle Travis). It is often played in country, folk, rock, and many other types of music.

Look at the basic patterns below and note how the right-hand thumb is being used, creating a somewhat different feel than arpeggios. The high E string is often played with your 2nd finger (m) instead of the usual 3rd finger (a) in this style. However, experiment with both fingers and choose the one most comfortable and natural for you. The fingering varies from one player to another in this style. Some incorporate all four fingers (p, i, m, a) while some use only *two* fingers (p & i)!

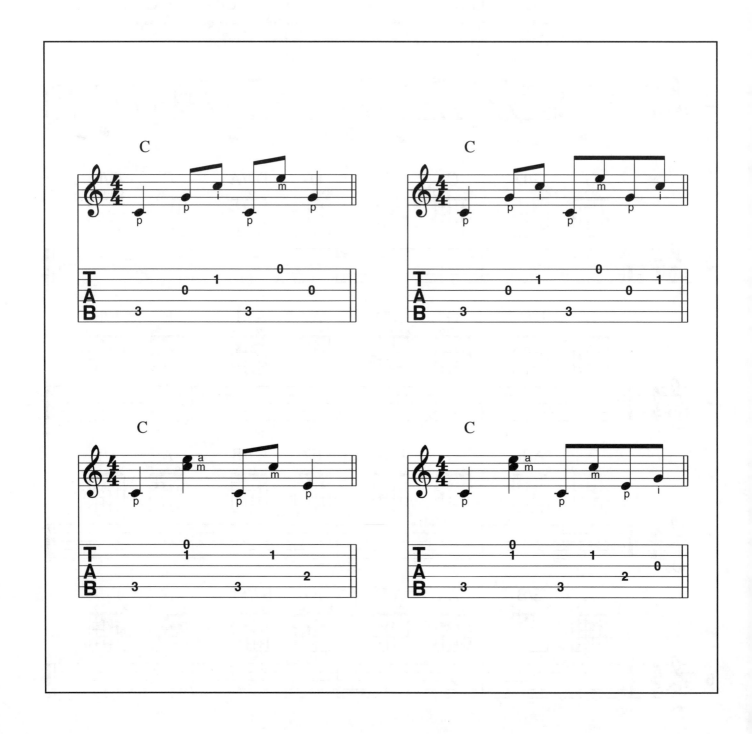

Slash chords, as mentioned earlier, are often used to create a certain bass movement in a chord progression. One possible use is to create a *descending* bass line as shown below in several different keys. Go over each chord carefully first and practice making a smooth transition from one chord to another.

5-3

Here are some more finger-picking patterns for you to play. Two of the patterns below are presented in sixteenth notes. Strive for a steady rhythm and time.

Although perhaps not used as often as a descending bass line, another way to incorporate slash chords in a chord progression is to create *an ascending* or *static* bass movement as shown below.

5·4

Below you will find two Carter Family Style and two finger-picking patterns with a hammer-on or pull-off. Keep practicing slowly until you can play each pattern comfortably.

As shown in the example, practice the following exercises in both the Carter Family and finger-picking styles adding hammer-ons and pull-offs.

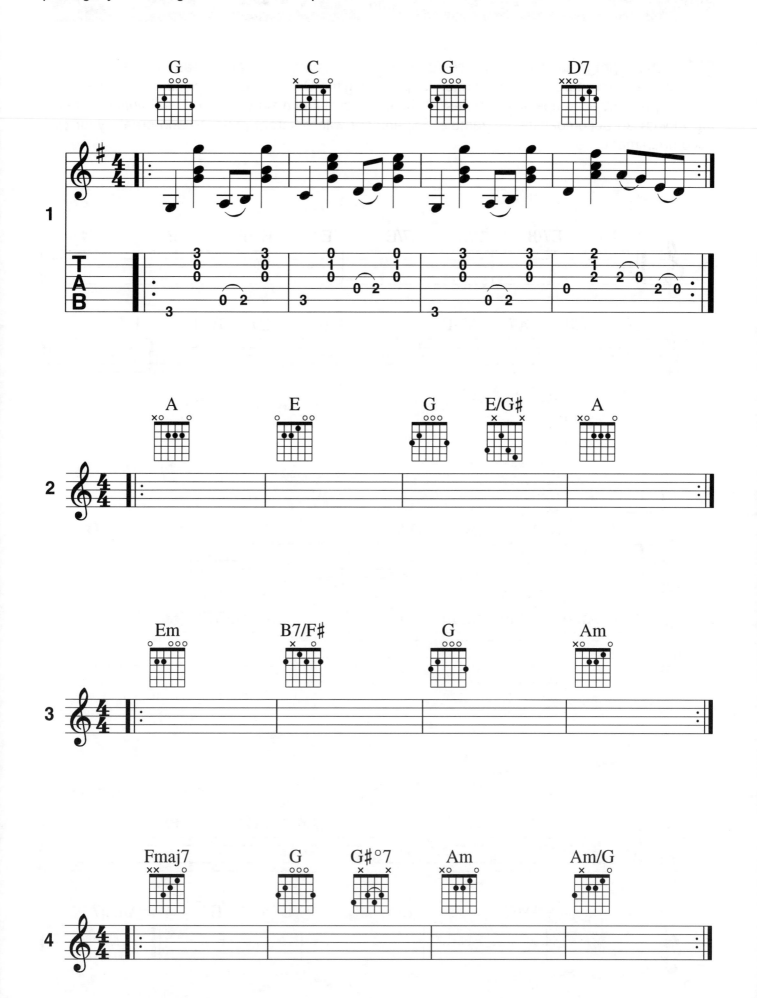

CHAPTER 5 REVIEW

The chord progressions below include some of the chords you have learned in this chapter. The first two progressions are written for practicing the Carter Family Style, but feel free to write out and play any accompaniment styles. At the end, you'll find a song, *When The Saints Go Marching In* with an accompaniment example. Experiment with different patterns and create your own accompaniment.

1

E7   E7/B   A7   A7/E   E7   E7/B   B7   B7F♯

E7   E7/B   A7   A7/E   B7   B7F♯   E7   E7/B   E7

2

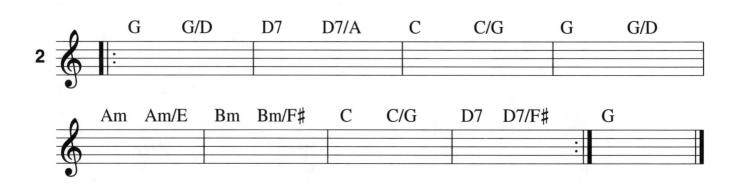

G   G/D   D7   D7/A   C   C/G   G   G/D

Am   Am/E   Bm   Bm/F♯   C   C/G   D7   D7/F♯   G

3

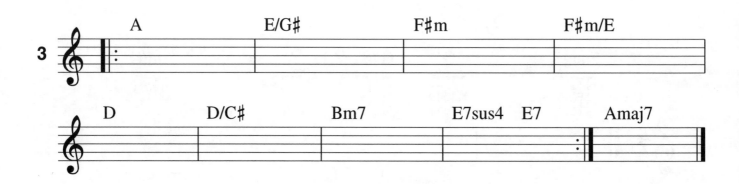

A   E/G♯   F♯m   F♯m/E

D   D/C♯   Bm7   E7sus4   E7   Amaj7

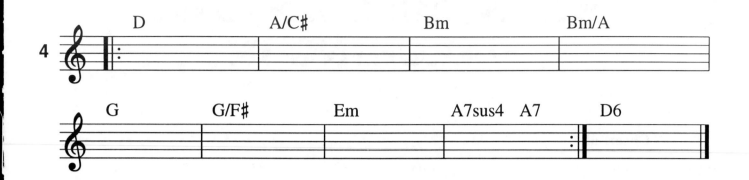

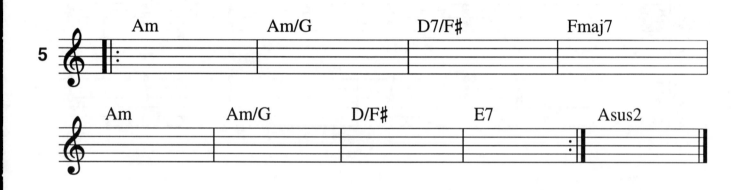

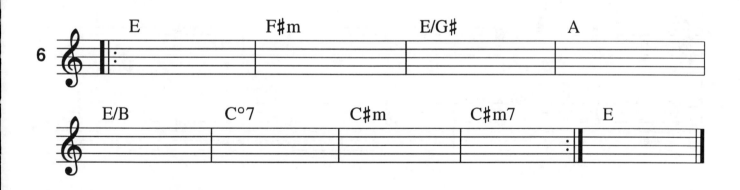

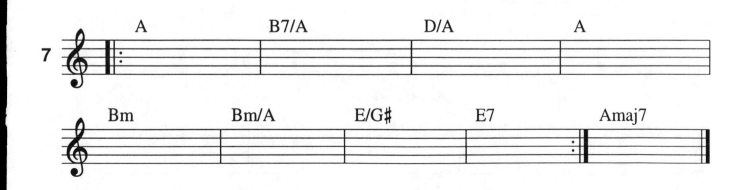

WHEN THE SAINTS GO MARCHING IN

Cheerfully

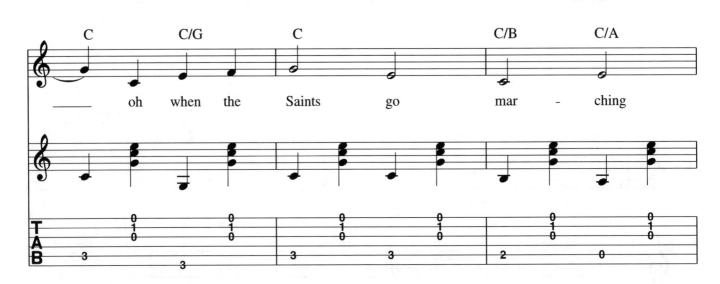

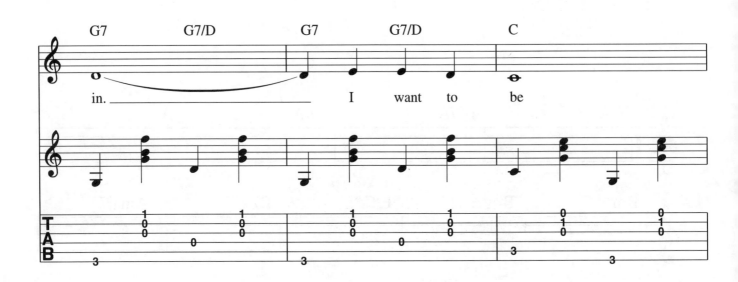

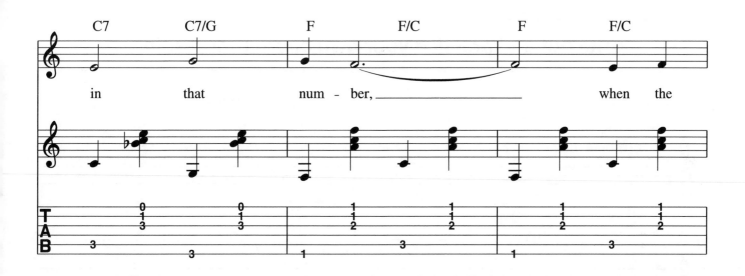

in   that   num - ber,_____ when   the

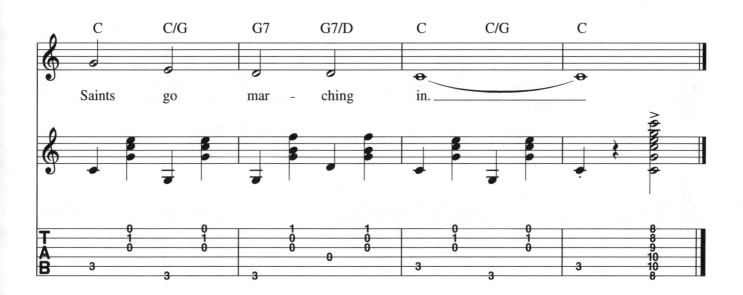

Saints   go   mar   -   ching   in._____

Additional Lyrics

2. And when they crown Him King of kings,
   And when they crown Him King of kings,
   I want to be in that number,
   When they crown Him King of kings.

3. And when they pave those streets with gold,
   And when they pave those streets with gold,
   I want to be in that number,
   When they pave those streets with gold.

Write out and practice your own chord progressions.

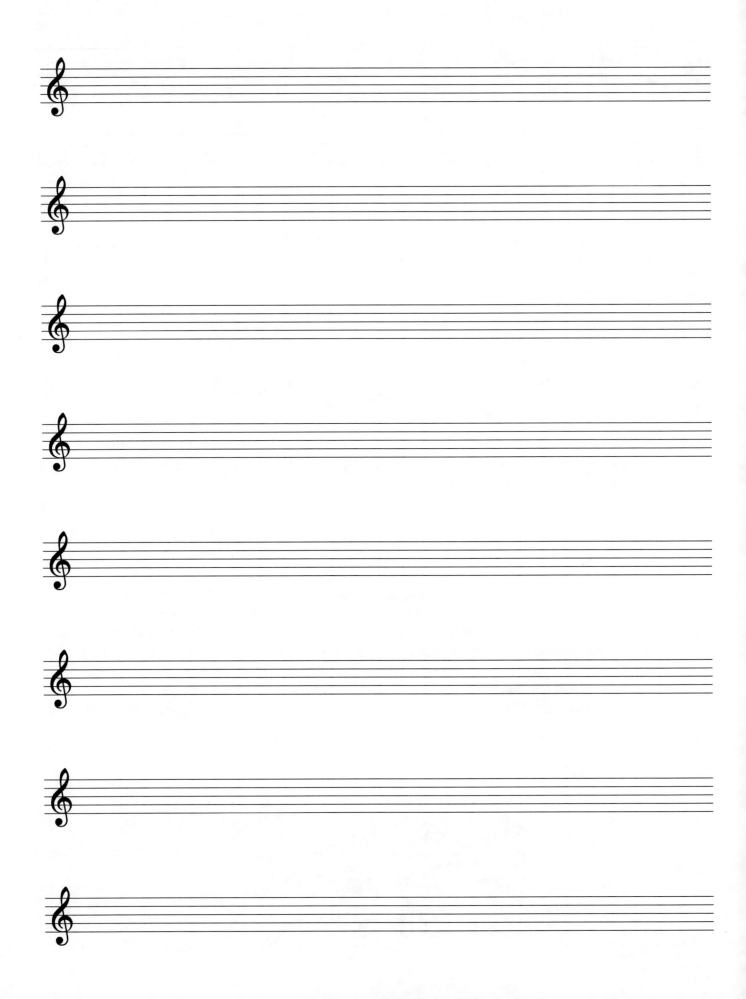

WHAT'S NEXT?

Now that you have finished this book, you should have gained a good foundation of guitar chords and basic accompaniment styles. Here are some suggestions regarding what you can do next:

1. Go back to each exercise and play it in different accompaniment styles than you played it initially. The exercises in the strumming sections, for example, can be played instead with any of the fingerstyles. Likewise, try any of the strumming patterns on the exercises from the fingerstyle sections.

2. Choose several of your favorite strumming and fingerstyle patterns and modify or combine them in any way you like thus creating *your own* patterns.

3. Practice each tune provided in this book until you can play it by memory. Then, pick and play as many other songs as you can each day from a fake or song book you have; if you do not presently have one, you can either borrow it from your local library or buy one. Play a song using any of the strumming patterns or fingerstyles, or make a contrast by combining two styles; very often the mood or the style of a song dictates which style to use, but ultimately it is *your* choice.

4. A chord can be played in several different ways on the guitar. Although each chord voicing presented in this book is popular and most frequently used, you are free to alter it by adding or subtracting notes from the chord. Experiment with as many ways as possible and eventually you may come up with many of *your own original chords*! For more different chords or variations and accompaniment styles, refer to *More Guitar Chords and Accompaniment (ISBN: 1-891370-11-1)* and *Jazz Guitar Chords and Accompaniment (ISBN: 1-891370-07-3)*.

5. Review all the materials from this book *regularly*.

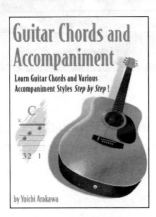

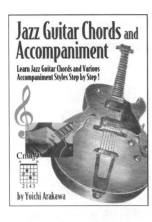

QUESTIONNAIRE

Thank you for your purchase of *Guitar Chords and Accompaniment (2nd ed).* Your suggestions, questions and comments are greatly appreciated. Please take the time to fill out this questionnaire and send it to: **SIX STRINGS MUSIC PUBLISHING, PO Box 7718, Torrance, CA 90504-9118.**

1. Where did you purchase this book?

2. How long have you been playing the guitar?

3. If you are a teacher, how long have you been teaching? What other books have you been using?

4. Which music magazines do you read regularly?

5. What music books (instructional or personal folios) do you use and like?

6. What kinds of music books would you like to see in the future?

7. What is your favorite type of music? Who is your favorite musician or music group?

8. Comments or suggestions regarding this book:

NAME: _____ **AGE:** _____

ADDRESS: _____

CITY: _____ **STATE:** _____ **ZIP:** _____

ORDER FORM

Item #	Titles	Qty	Price	Subtotal
			$	$
			$	$
			$	$
			$	$
			Subtotal	$
			CA resident—7.00% sales tax **LA county—8.00% sales tax**	$
			Shipping & handling ($5.50 for the first book, add $1.25 for each additional copy)	$
			TOTAL	$

PAYMENT

❑ **CHECK** or **MONEY ORDER** (U.S. ONLY)

Please send this order form with your check or money order to:

SIX STRINGS MUSIC PUBLISHING, P.O. Box 7718, Torrance, CA 90504-9118

❑ **CREDIT CARD:** ○ **Visa** ○ **MasterCard** ○ **American Express**

Mail this order form *or* fax it to **310-324-8544** *or* call toll-free **800-784-0203**.

Card number: _____

Name on card: _____ Exp. date: _____

❑ **INTERNET:** You can also order on-line at: **http://www.sixstringsmusicpub.com**

Prices subject to change without notice. No C.O.D. orders please.

MAILING ADDRESS

NAME: _____ AGE: _____

ADDRESS: _____

CITY: _____ STATE: _____ ZIP: _____

TEL: _____ E-MAIL: _____